AF615197

Phaidon Press Limited
140 Kensington Church Street
London W8 4BN

First published in Great Britain 1992

ISBN 0 7148 2818 1

A CIP catalogue record for this book is available from the British Library

Front cover materials courtesy of London Graphic Centre.

Printed in Spain

Learn to draw with

Markers

Materials, skills and step-by-step projects

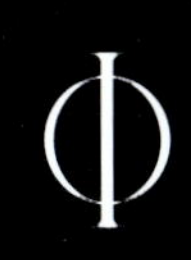

Markers

Learning to use markers

This book has been designed to help you learn how to draw with markers (also called fibre-tipped or felt-tipped pens). It tells you about the materials you need and explains the various skills used to create different effects. Start by reading about the basic skills, then follow the step-by-step projects later in the book to practise what you've learned. Any terms you're not sure of are explained in the glossary at the back of the book.

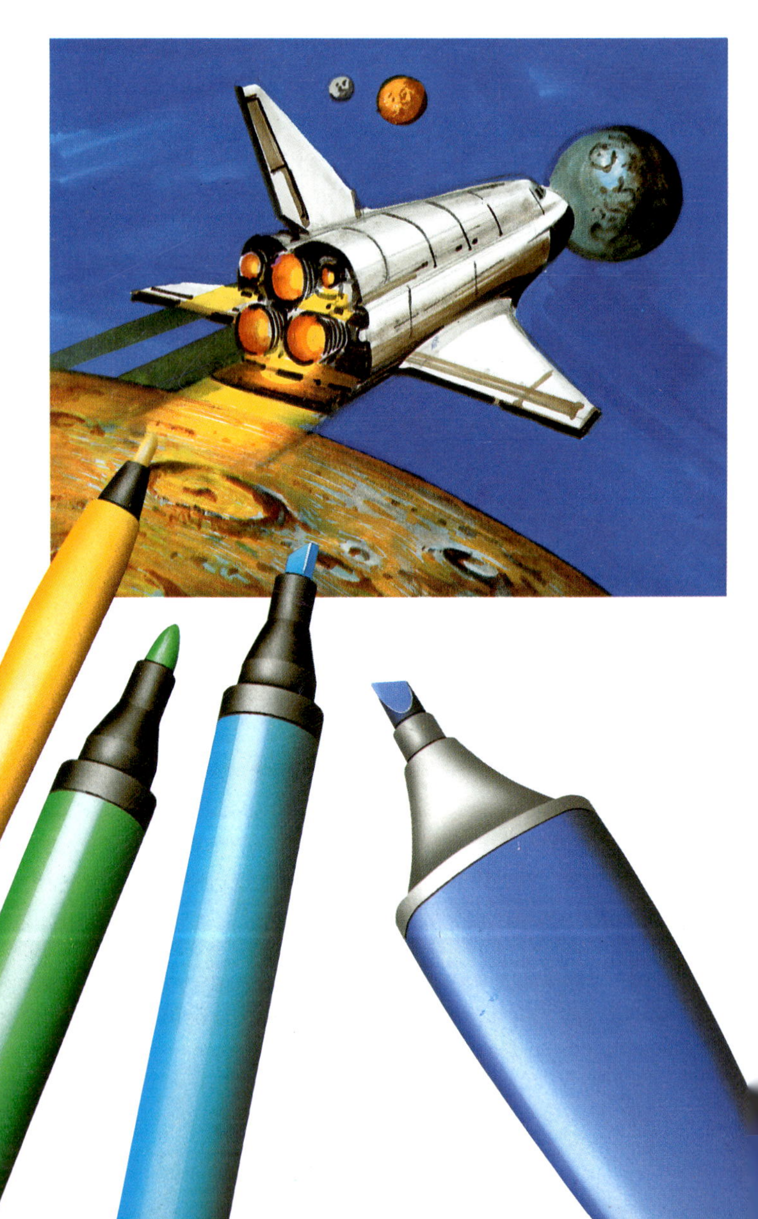

This book is divided into three parts: the first part tells you about the materials you need; the second part explains the skills for using markers; the third part contains step-by-step projects to follow.

You can buy many different types of markers in a wide range of colours.

How they work

Drawing with markers

The ink in markers is transparent, in the same way as watercolour paint. When you draw with a marker, you can see pencil lines or the colours underneath through the ink. Unlike watercolour paints, which are diluted with water, you draw directly on to the paper with markers.

When you are drawing with markers and felt-tips remember:

- use the lighter colours first
- white is not usually used; you can use the colour of the paper to give you white areas
- you can mix colours by putting one on top of another on the paper

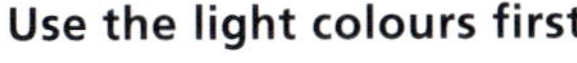

Use the light colours first

Use the dark colours afterwards

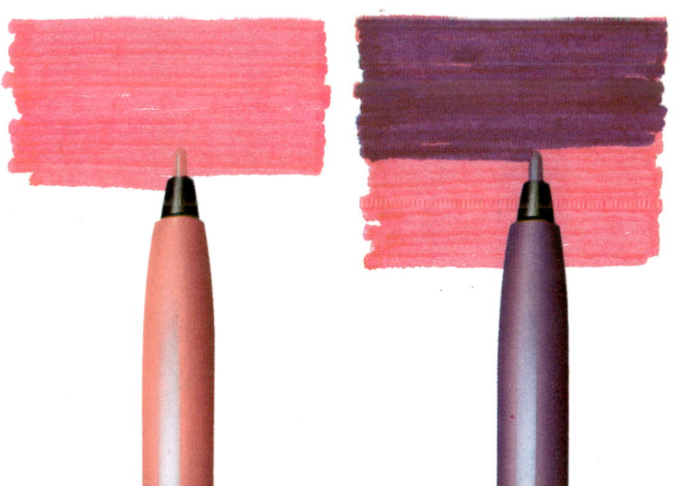

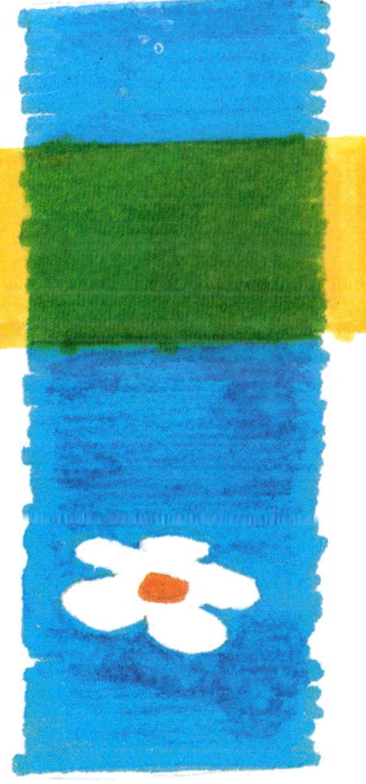

Marker colours are transparent. If you put yellow on to a blue background, you will create green.

White areas can be outlined beforehand on the paper.

Markers

What is a marker?

Markers and fibre tips have a small tank inside containing a fibre wick which is soaked in ink. A tube at the end of the wick carries the ink to the tip of the pen. The pen's cap stops the ink evaporating.

Types of markers

The ink in markers can be water-based or spirit-based. Spirit-based inks dry faster than water-based ones; this is one of the reasons that illustrators who work in advertising use them.

Inside a marker

A Tank
B Felt wick
C Internal tube
D Tip
E Head
F Cap

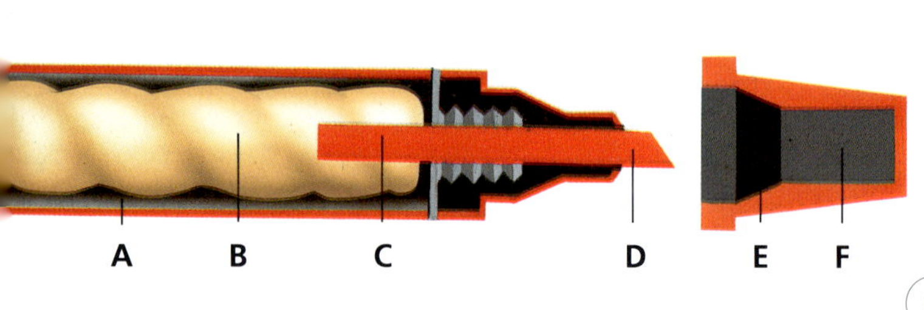

Markers have different types of tip:

1 Fine-tipped pens. These are used for outlines, or colouring in small spaces.

2 Round-tipped pens (standard or broad). These make rather thick lines and are good for colouring in large areas.

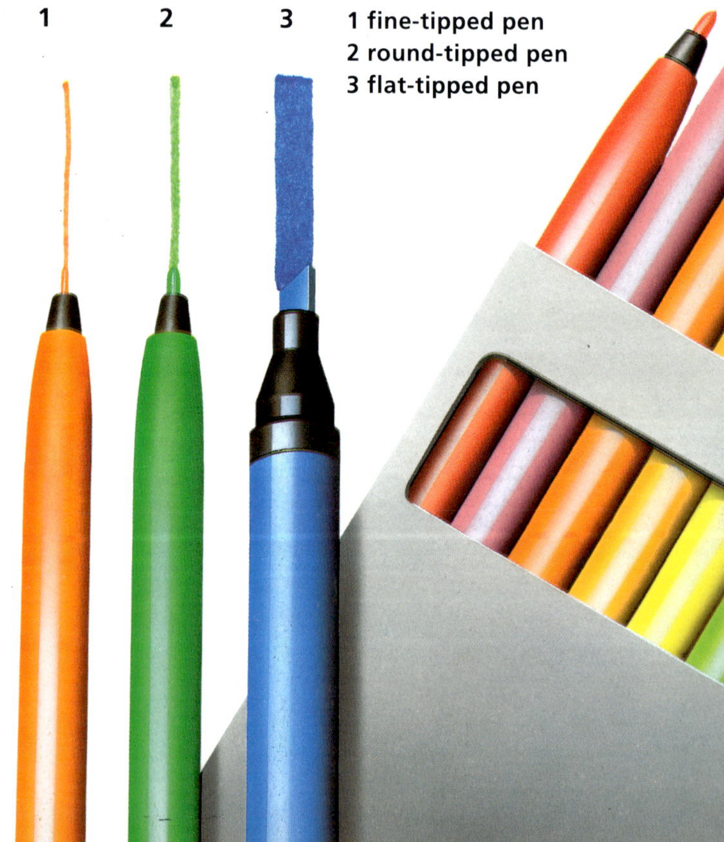

1 fine-tipped pen
2 round-tipped pen
3 flat-tipped pen

How to choose them

3 Flat-tipped pens (fine, standard or broad). These are good for colouring large areas or making thick lines.

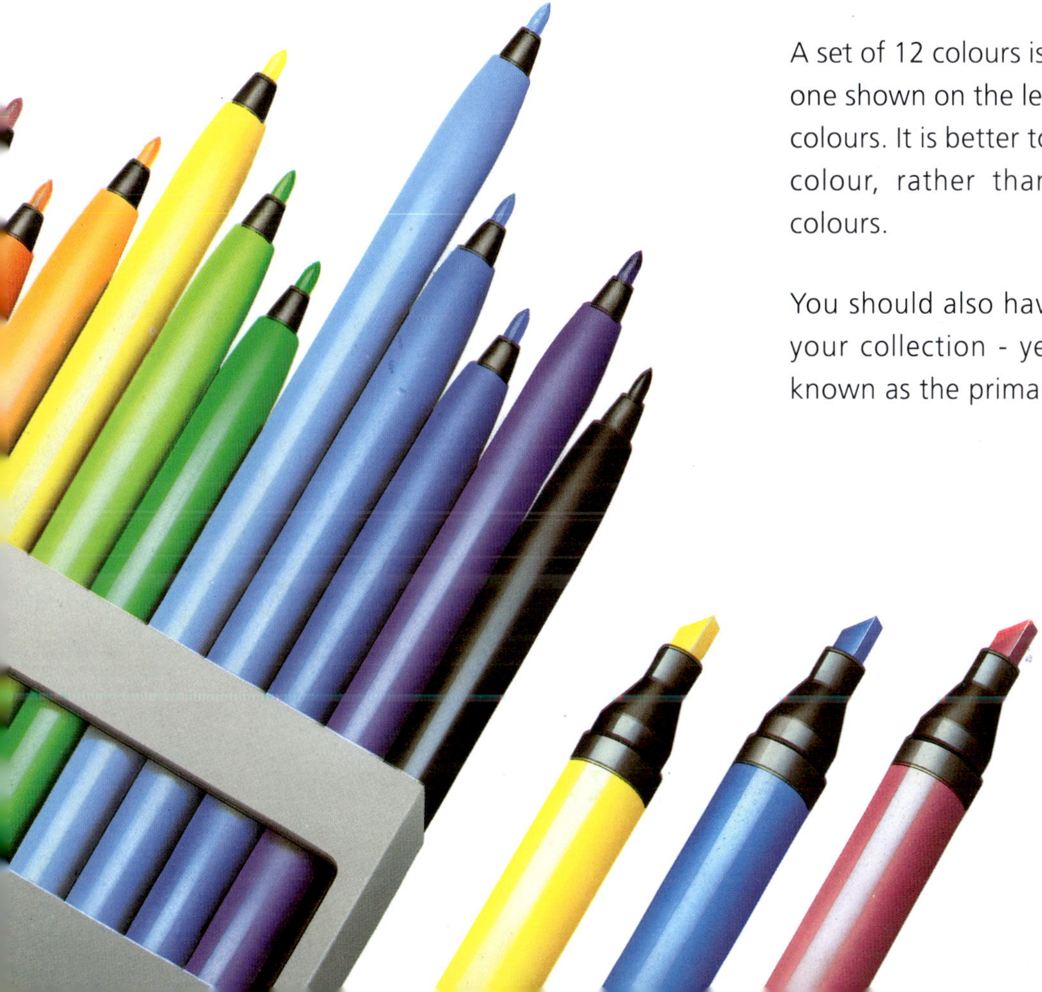

For the projects in this book you will need a set of water-based markers with a round, standard-size tip. You will also need at least three flat-tipped pens.

Choosing colours

A set of 12 colours is plenty to start with, such as the one shown on the left, which includes dark and light colours. It is better to have several tones of the same colour, rather than a wide variety of different colours.

You should also have three flat-tipped felt pens in your collection - yellow, blue and red. These are known as the primary colours.

What to draw on

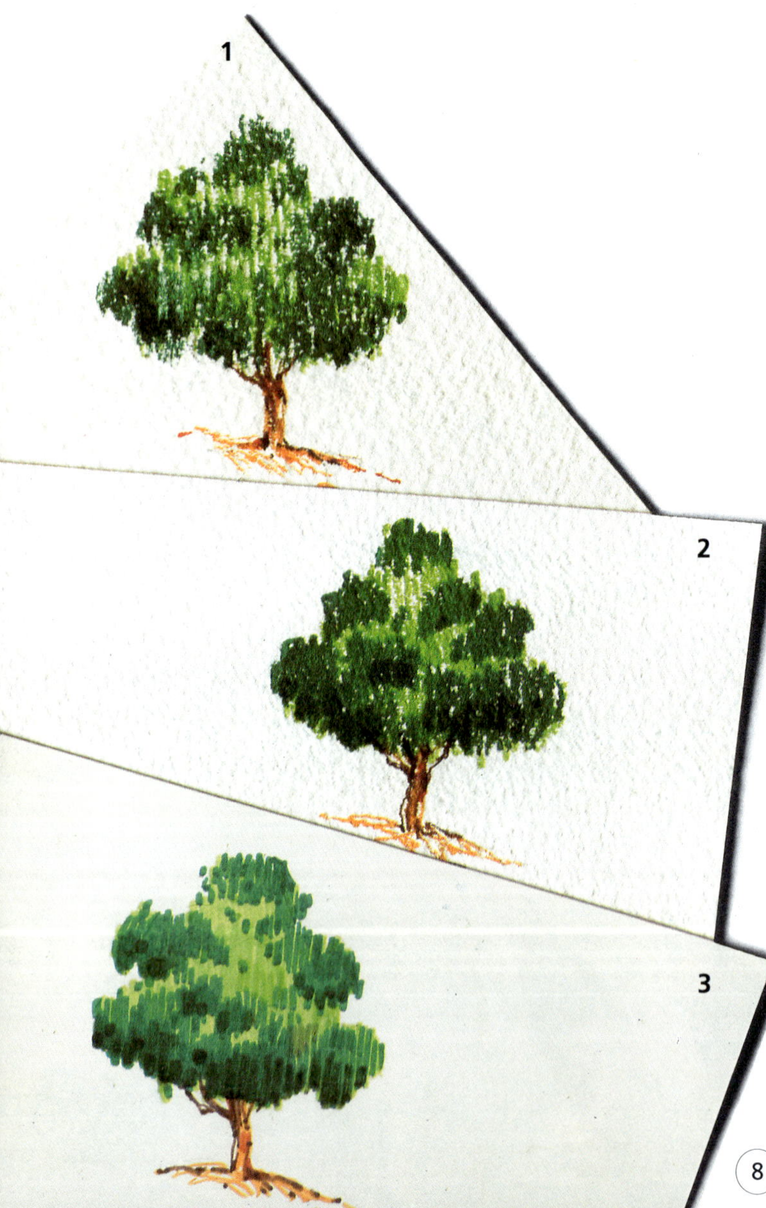

Some facts about paper

Different types of paper are described according to their weight and texture.

The weight of a paper describes how much a square metre of paper weighs. The thicker the paper the heavier it is. Paper which weighs 80 grammes per square metre is very thin; on the other hand, paper which weighs 350 grammes is as thick as card.

The texture is the roughness or smoothness of the paper, which is described as its grain. There are high, medium and low grain papers. There are also types of paper which are completely smooth and have no grain.

Papers ***1*** *and* ***2*** *are textured. They are not suitable for drawing with markers. Glossy papers (such as* ***3****) which have no grain are best for this kind of work.*

How to choose paper

Choosing the right paper

The best paper for drawing with felt-tips and markers should have three qualities:

- It should be smooth, with very little or no grain, so that the pen can move easily over its surface
- It should be absorbent, so the ink doesn't run
- It should have a glossy surface so that the ink doesn't dry before you have finished colouring an area

A smooth paper weighing about 200 grammes is ideal. You can buy single sheets measuring 50 x 70 cm which you can cut to the right size, or buy the paper in pads.

Special papers

There are papers specially made for drawing on with markers, which can be used with both water-based and spirit-based pens.

These papers have a glossy surface, an absorbent layer underneath, and a waterproof layer at the bottom which stops the ink soaking through the paper.

Special paper for markers

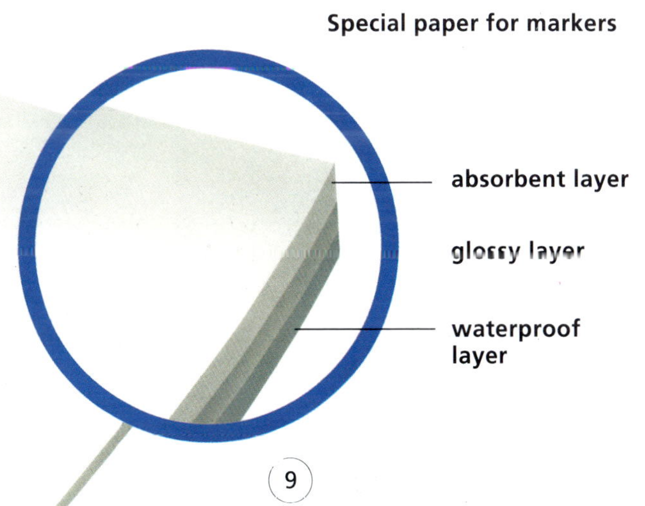

The three layers of this paper are:

- *a glossy layer, over which the pen can move easily*
- *an absorbent layer, so the ink doesn't run*
- *a waterproof layer, which prevents the ink from soaking through the paper*

Making work easy

Containers for your markers

It is a good idea to store your markers in two containers - they could be pots or jam-jars - so that they are always to hand.

Keep the cool range of colours in one container. These are greens, blues and mauves. In the other put the warm colours - yellows, oranges, and reds. Separating the two colour ranges will help you work more quickly.

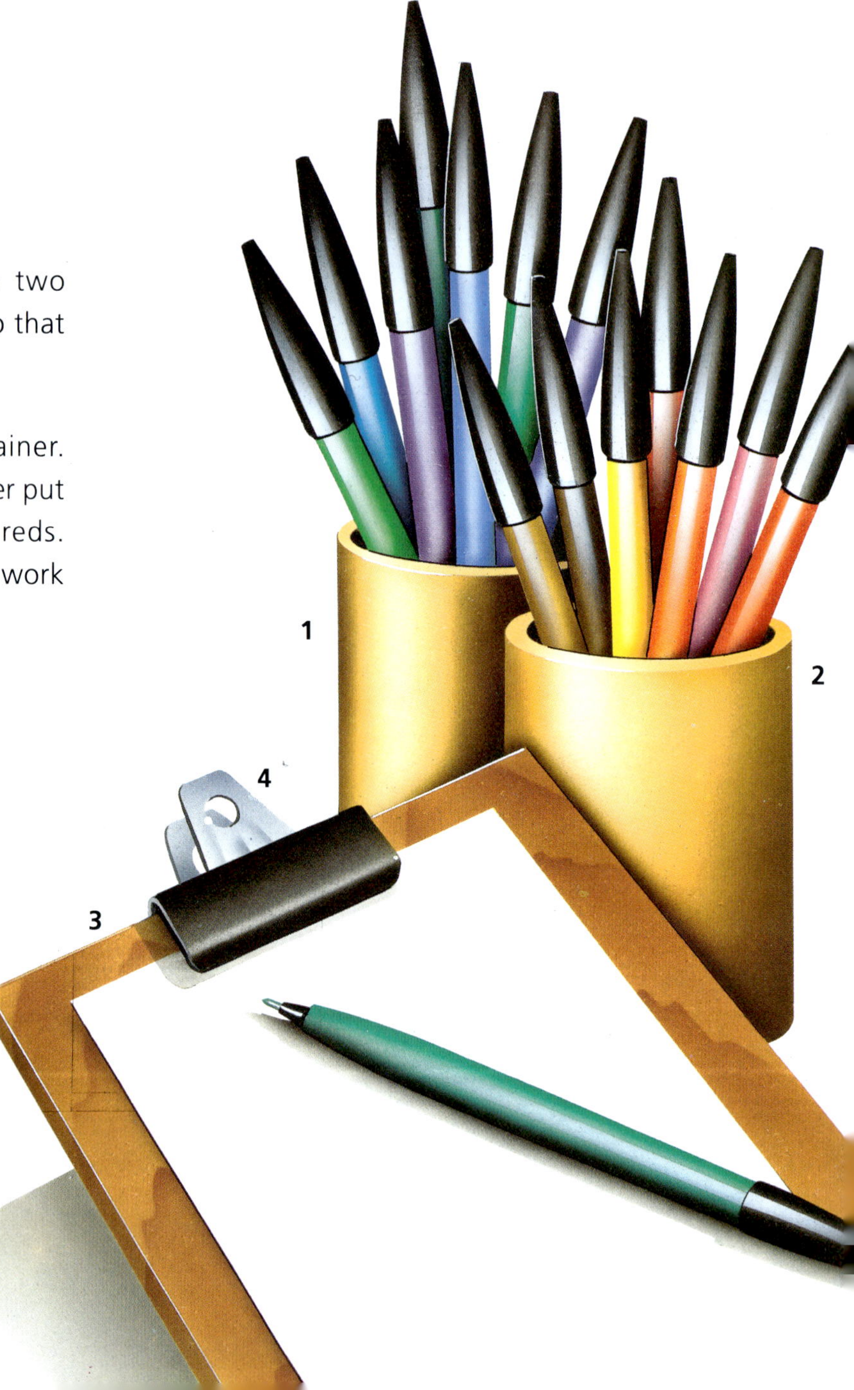

1 Pot containing warm colours
2 Pot containing cool colours
3 Clipboard for leaning on
4 Bulldog clip to keep the paper in place
5 Rubber (only used for pencil sketches)
6 Drawing pins to hold large sheets of paper in place
7 Lead pencils for drawing
8 Drawing pad

Other tools & materials

A wooden drawing board

It is a good idea to use a wooden drawing board measuring about 40 x 60 cm. Rest the board between your knees and the edge of the table you are working on so that you are comfortable when working.

Bulldog clips and drawing pins

A bulldog clip is useful for holding small pieces of paper in place. If you are using larger sheets pin them on to your drawing board with drawing pins.

Pencils

Remember that the ink of a marker will not cover the pencil lines of a sketch. For your initial drawing use hard (H) or semi-hard (HB) pencils.

Rubber

A plastic rubber is useful when working on your initial pencil drawings.

A drawing pad

A standard-size drawing pad is ideal for making sketches before starting your final picture.

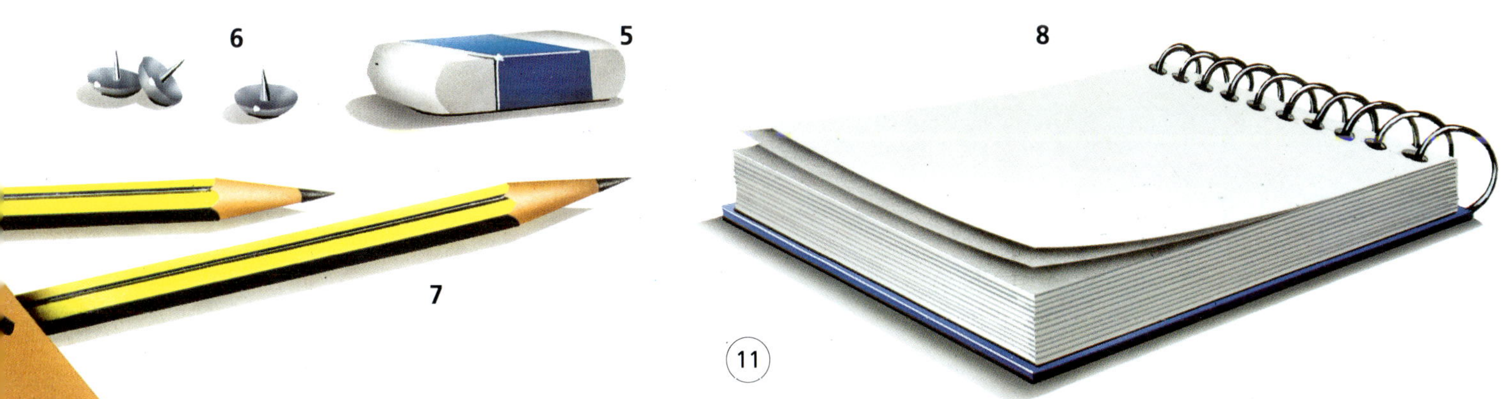

Drawing skills

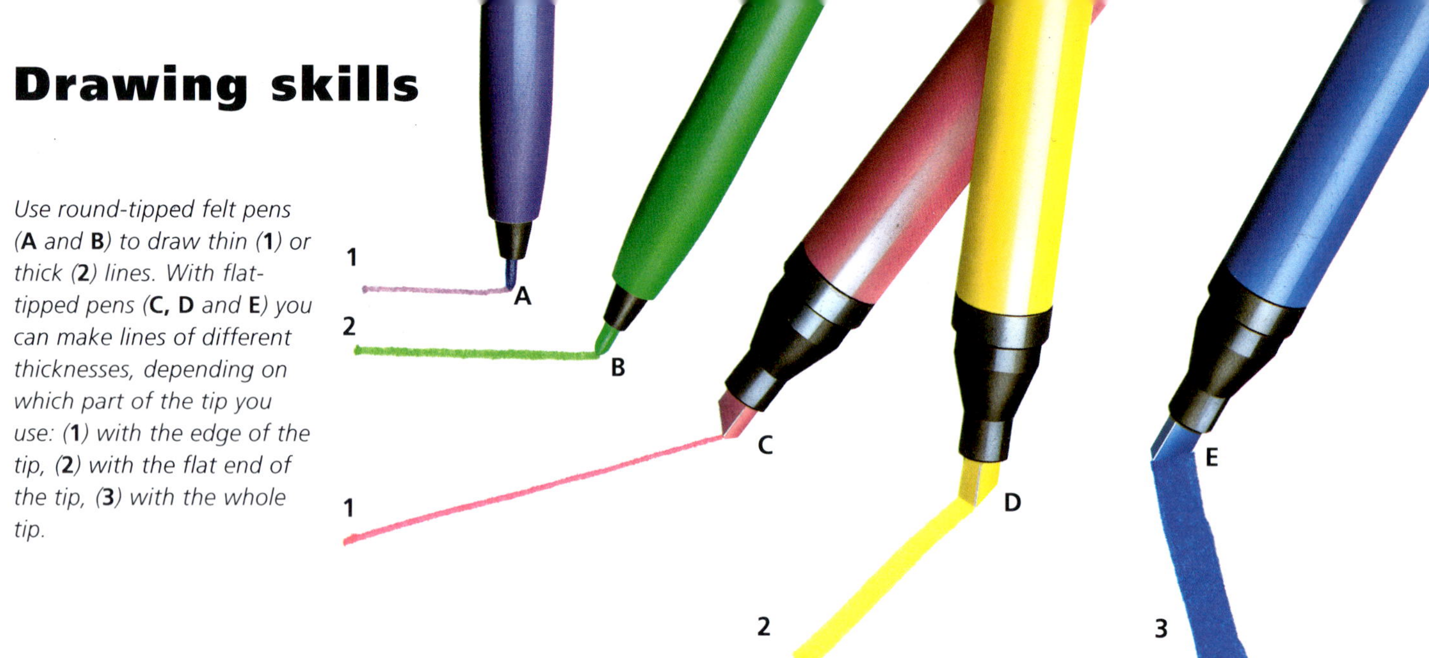

*Use round-tipped felt pens (**A** and **B**) to draw thin (**1**) or thick (**2**) lines. With flat-tipped pens (**C, D** and **E**) you can make lines of different thicknesses, depending on which part of the tip you use: (**1**) with the edge of the tip, (**2**) with the flat end of the tip, (**3**) with the whole tip.*

Holding felt pens

The way in which you hold a marker depends on the type of line you want to make.

If you want to draw details or a thin line, you should hold the pen as if you were going to write with it. If you want to colour in a large area, it is better to grip the pen with your whole hand.

Drawing with round-tipped pens

With a round-tipped pen you can draw lines as thick or thin as the tip will allow, or you can use the side of the top to fill in large areas.

Drawing with flat-tipped pens

These pens can be used in different ways:

- use the edge of the tip to draw thin lines
- use the flat end to create thick lines
- press part of the flat end at an angle to fill in large areas

Useful tips

- Always keep your wrist straight when moving the pen. Your arm and the pen should move together.
- Move the pen over the paper with continuous strokes, without stopping or being rough. This will help you to draw an even line, and will make sure that you do not leave more ink in some areas than others.

Use markers in the same way as coloured pencils - with continuous strokes and even pressure, so that the colour is even.

Rubbing out

The ink of a marker is absorbed by the paper, so it is almost impossible to rub out. If you make a mistake you can try using a rubber on the ink straight away, but you may dirty the area you try to rub out, or damage the paper if you rub too hard. So it is best not to use a rubber with markers.

Rubbing out fibre-tips and markers is not a good idea. You may be able to remove some colour, but you risk leaving a dirty mark on the paper.

Drawing skills

Creating an even background

This is how to colour in large areas with markers.

Use a pencil to draw a square 10 x 10 cm. Then start filling in the square with straight lines, holding the pen at an angle.

Draw the lines next to each other keeping the same pressure on the tip of the pen all the time. You will need to work quickly to make even tones in all the lines before the ink dries.

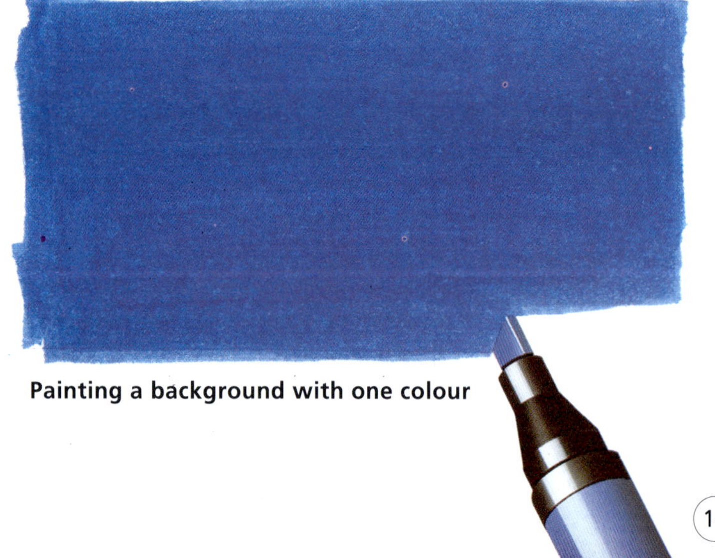

Painting a background with one colour

Different tones of a colour

Because the ink in a marker is transparent you can gradually darken the tone of a colour by putting one layer on top of another.

Start by drawing a rectangle and colouring it in with one colour. Then, in one section of the rectangle, add another layer of ink to make it darker.

Finally, add another layer in part of the same area. This will make this part even darker.

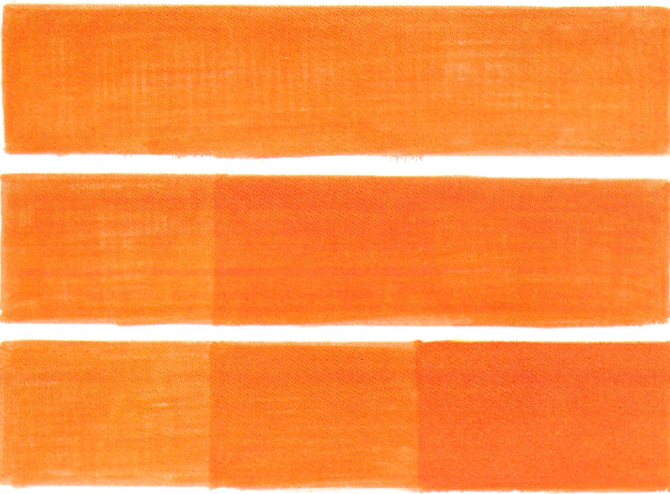

Drawing parallel lines

Artists often use a technique called parallel lines. This means covering the surface with lines or strokes which are parallel and next to each other.

All the lines must be drawn in the same direction: usually from top to bottom or from left to right.

When you begin practising, you will find that it is easier to draw vertical lines than horizontal ones.

Practise drawing parallel lines on scraps of paper, making sure that the lines do not overlap too much.

Combing or sweeping are other types of parallel lines which use the direction of the line to form the shape of what you are drawing.

Look at the pictures on this page, which were done with parallel lines and sweeping.

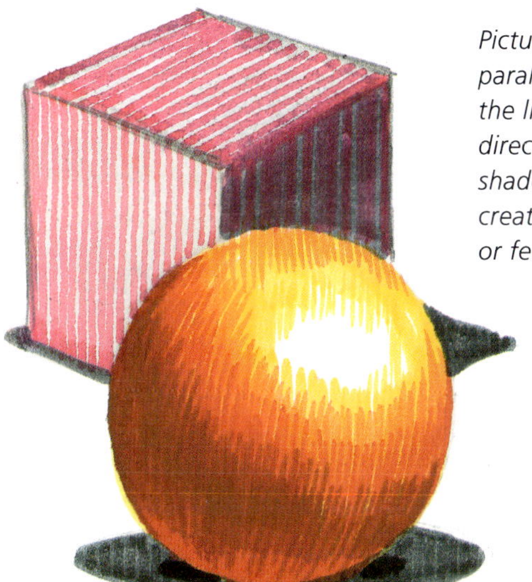

Pictures made up of parallel lines. See how the lines go in one direction and how the shadows have been created by drawing more or fewer lines.

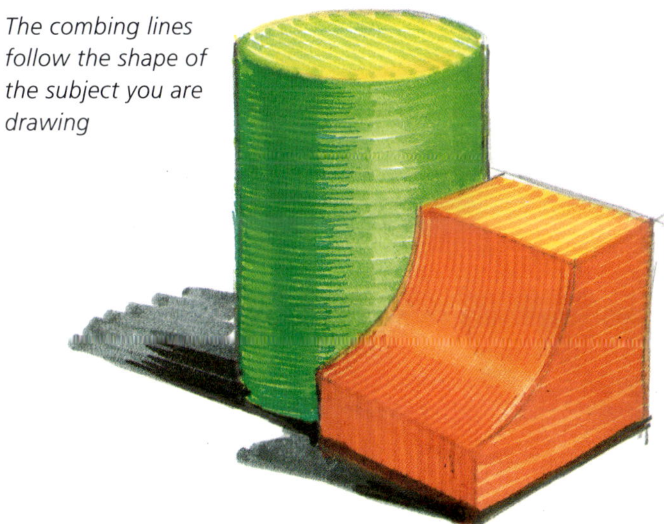

The combing lines follow the shape of the subject you are drawing

Drawing skills

Making gradations

When drawing with markers you can't create darker or lighter colours by pressing more heavily or lightly on the tip, as you can with coloured pencils.

To create a gradation you need to work with several tones (the more the better) of the same colour. You may need to buy markers individually in order to collect a good range of tones.

To create a gradation similar to the one on this page, draw a rectangle using a pencil and colour it in with a light tone.

Before the ink dries, put a darker colour next to the rectangle so that it overlaps the light tone. Then colour the overlapping area with the light tone to blend the colours together.

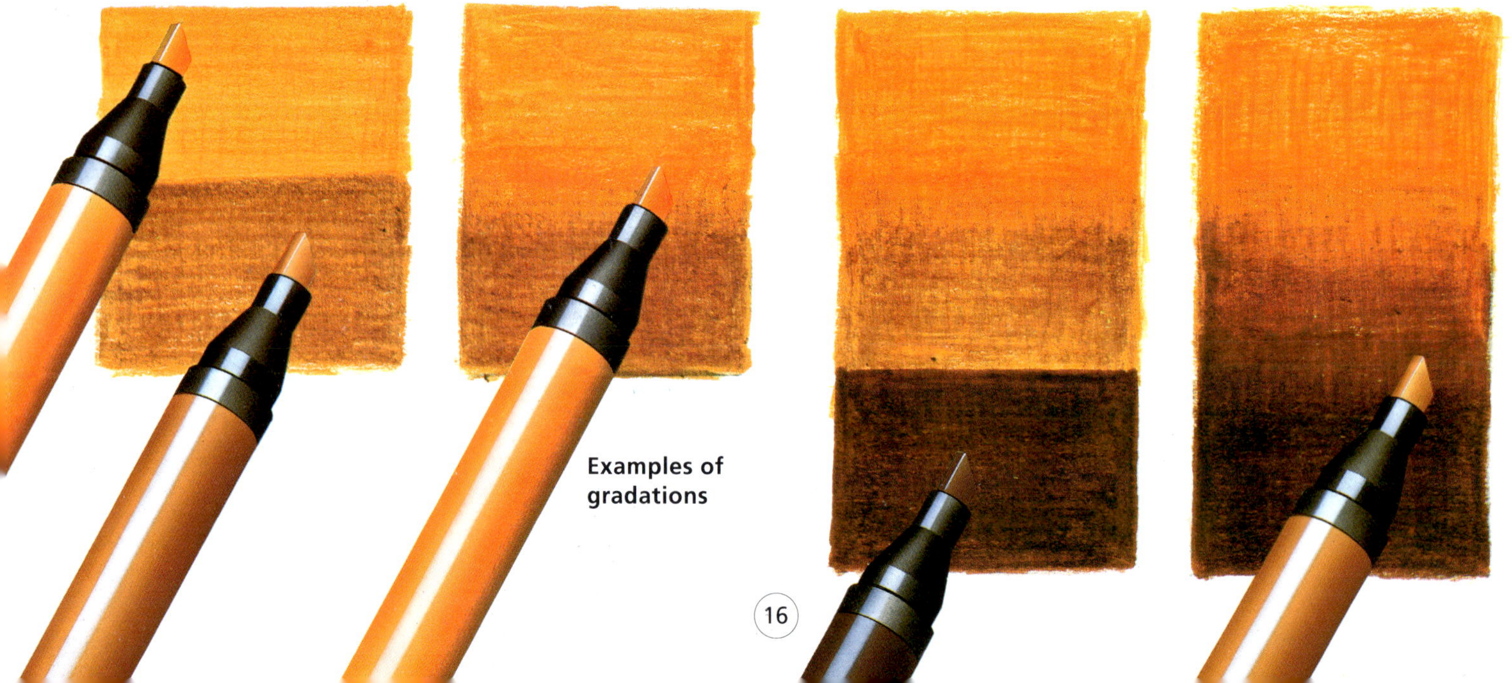

Examples of gradations

Blending colours

Blending is used to join colours next to each other to make a gradation, or when putting one colour on top of another when you are doing parallel lines.

You can only blend when the ink is still wet; it must be done before the first tone dries. You will need to go over the tones several times to achieve a good blend.

Colours next to each other

Blending with the lighter colour

Overlapping colours

To create a gradation you can overlap or add another layer of colour. But it is easy to overlap a new colour on to one already there when you don't want to. This may result in a colour you don't like.

This is how to stop this happening:

- First outline the areas of the different colours with a hard pencil
- Then outline the inside of each area to be coloured with the colour you are going to use
- When the ink is dry, colour in the outlined area

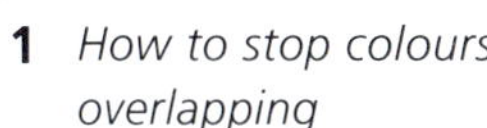

1 *How to stop colours overlapping*

1 *Outline the area with a marker*

2 *Fill it in with colour. This is the best way of painting different shapes so that the colours do not overlap*

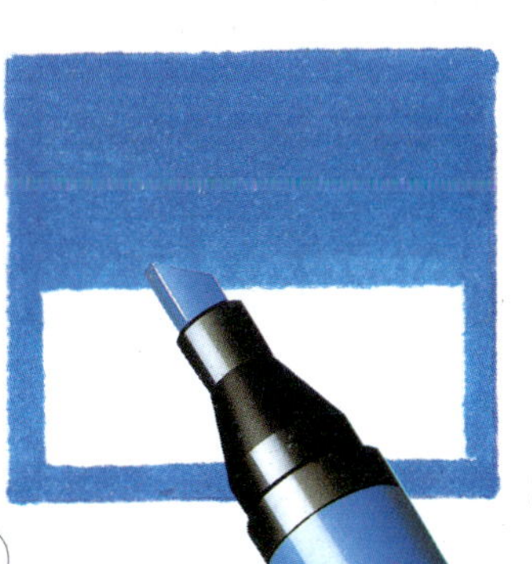

2

Drawing skills

Mixing colours

With markers you paint two or more colours on top of each other to create the mix you want.

Try practising colour mixing on scrap paper. Experimenting with different mixes will help you to create the colours you want in your future pictures.

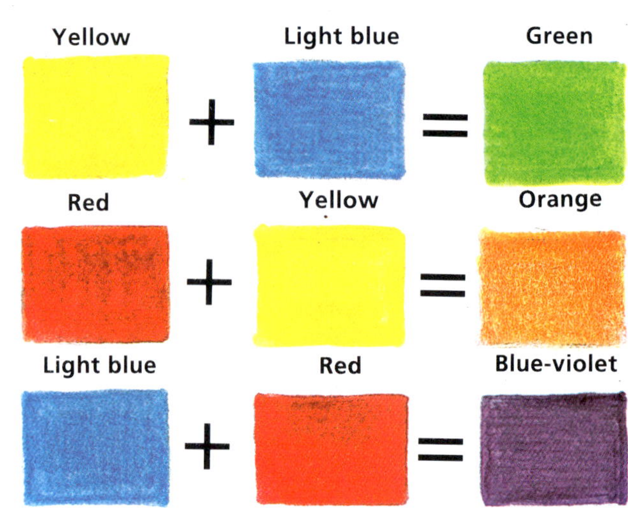

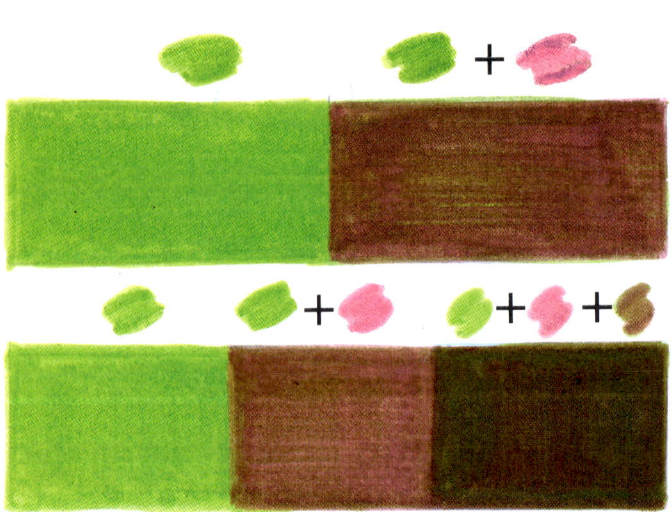

Above, a two-colour mix; this was the result of adding a third colour to a mixture of two colours.

The primary colours

The three most important colours in your set of pens are light blue, red and yellow. These are the primary colours, and by mixing these three you can create all the colours in nature.

If you mix the primary colours in pairs, you create three new colours: the secondary colours. If you mix a primary colour with a secondary colour you create even more colours, called tertiary colours: light green, dark green, dark blue, violet, crimson and orange.

The colour wheel

The colour wheel (or chromatic circle) is made up of 12 different colours.

The colours which are directly opposite one another on the colour wheel are called the complementary colours. You can see how the secondary colours (**S**) are made by mixing primary colours (**P**). The tertiary colours (**T**) are made by mixing a primary colour with the secondary colour which is next to it, on the right or the left.

Left, the secondary colours - green, orange and purple - all made by mixing pairs of primary colours.

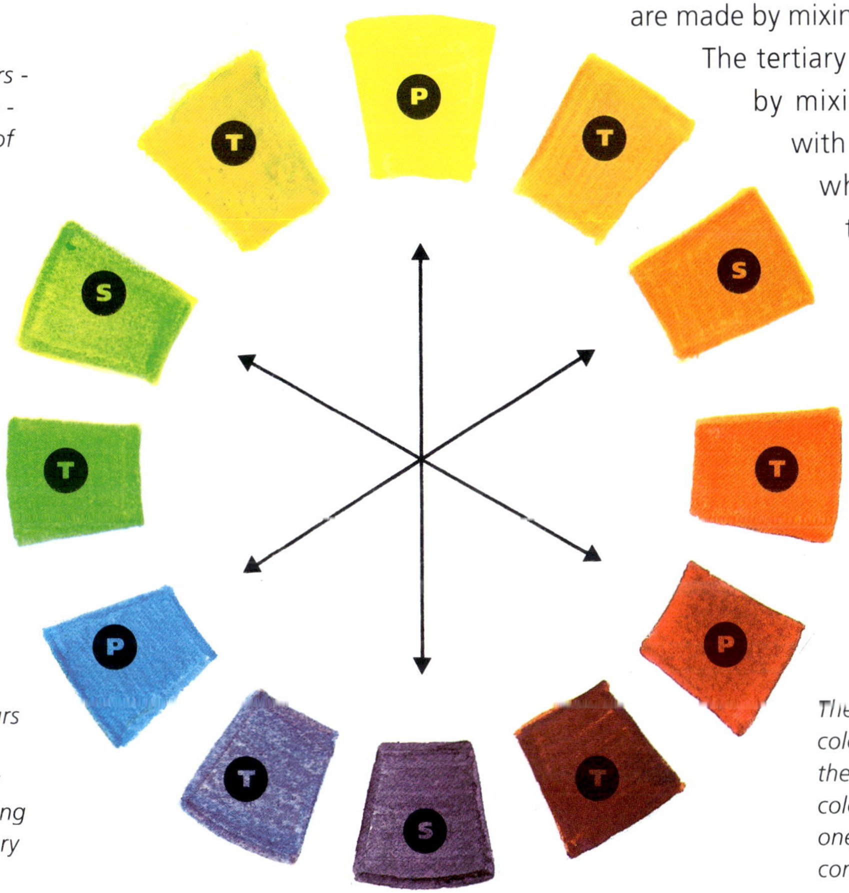

*The colour wheel on the right has 12 colours: the three primary colours (**P**), the three secondary colours (**S**) made by mixing the primaries, and six tertiary colours (**T**), made by mixing a primary with a secondary colour.*

The arrows inside the colour wheel point to the complementary colours: put next to one another they contrast strongly

First projects

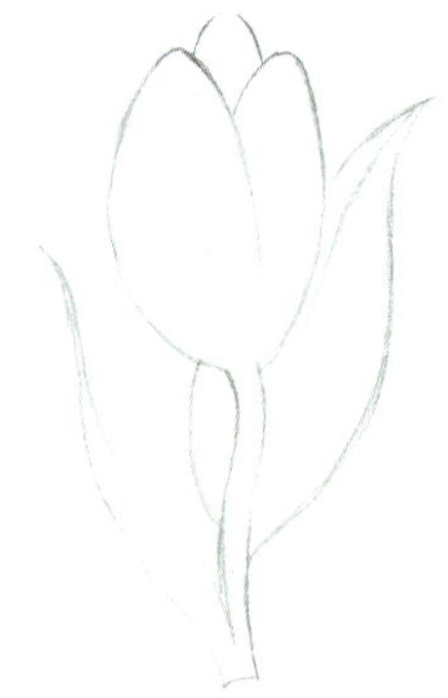

Drawing this flower will help you to practise colouring without overlapping the lines.

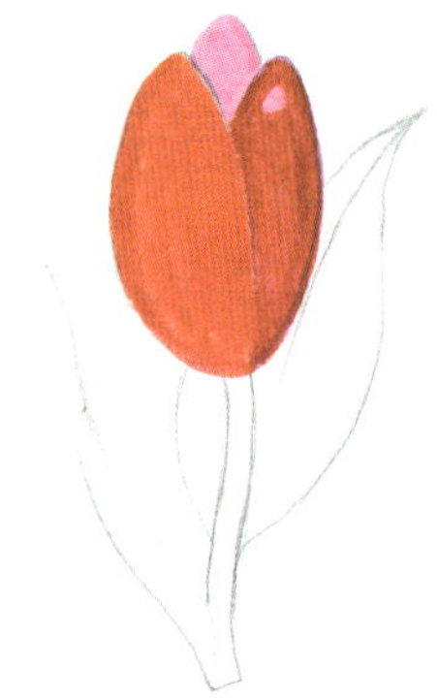

Outline the petals with a round-tipped pen and then colour them in.

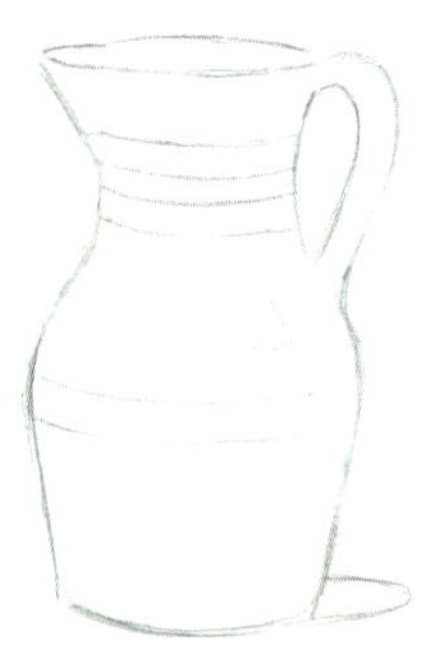

Draw the jug and outline its shape carefully. Mark in the highlights and shadows.

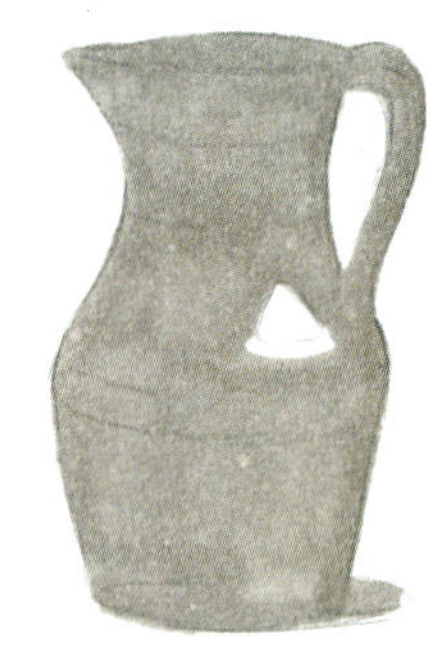

Colour in the jug with strokes going in the same direction, leaving the highlight area white.

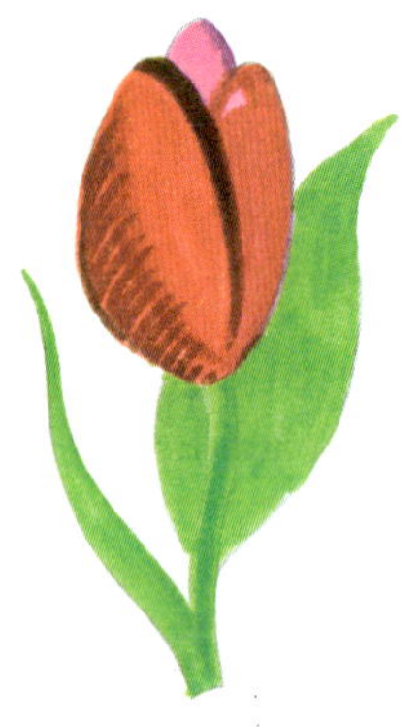

Do the same with the leaves; be careful not to let your outlines overlap.

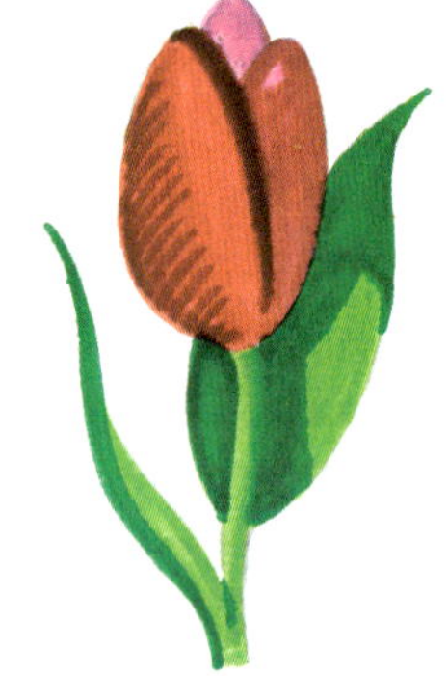

Add darker lines, without mixing the colour at the bottom, and then the light tones.

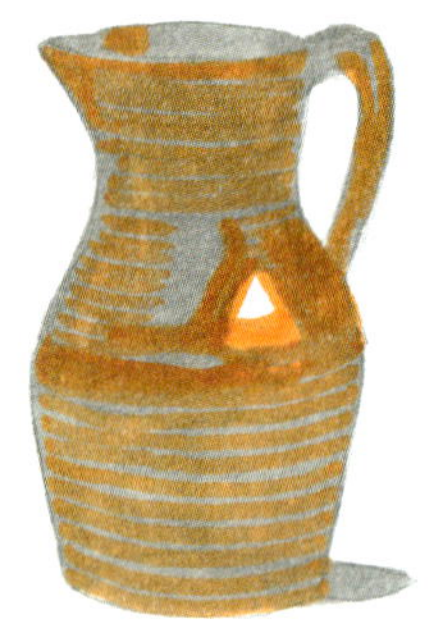

Use the combing technique and start on the shadows, working with the darkest tones.

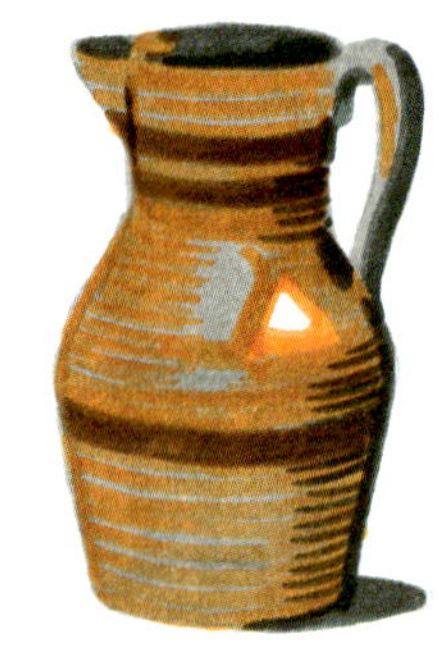

Finally, deepen the shadows and strengthen the sides of the jug.

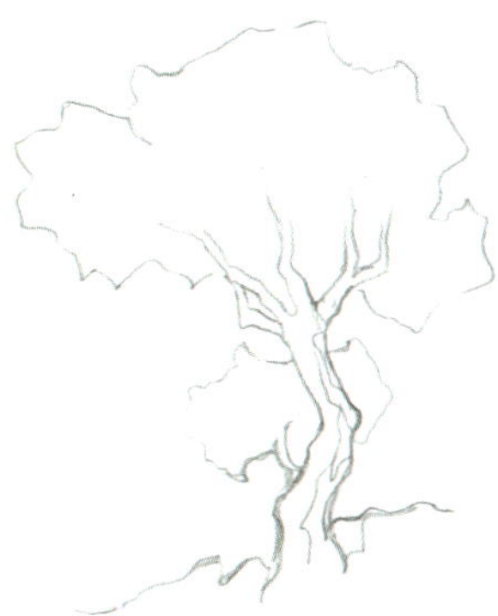

Continue to practise making visible lines. Draw the basic shape of the tree.

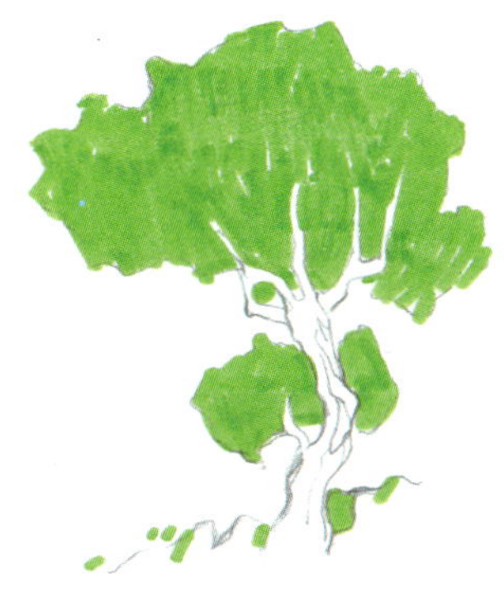

Colour in the tree tops and the area of shadow on the ground.

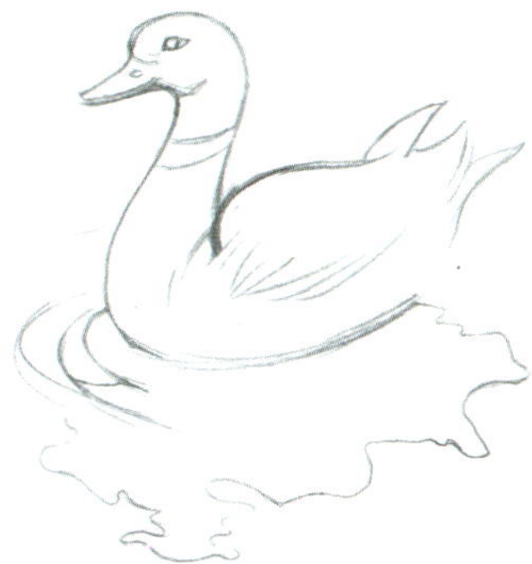

First draw the duck and its reflection on the water, outlinining each area of colour.

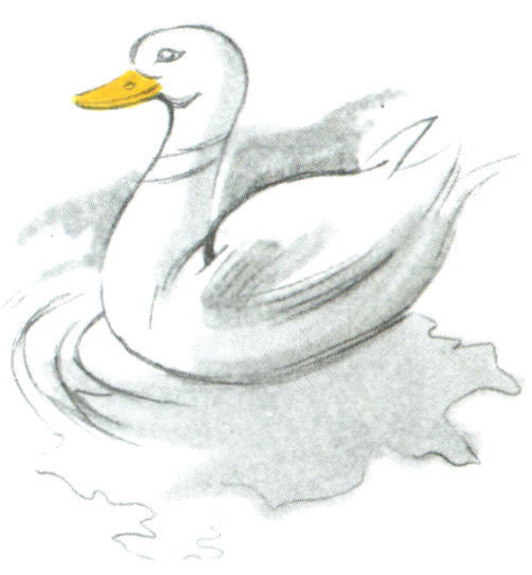

Start colouring with a light tone. Don't worry about going over the pencil lines.

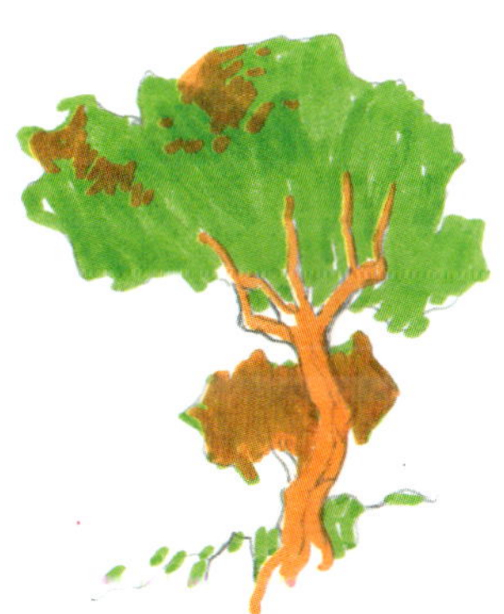

Use a darker tone on the tree in the foreground and put some lines on the trunk.

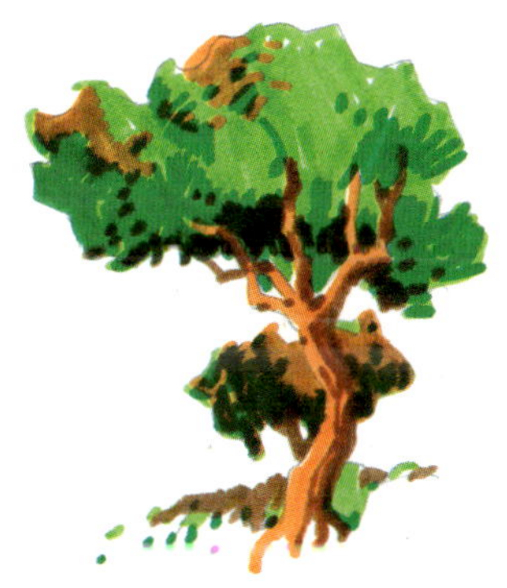

Touch up the tree tops and the trunk with dark lines.

Now add dark tones to the duck's head, neck and feathers. Do a gradation on the reflection on the water.

Strengthen some of the lines in the water and gradate the colour of the duck's head and the reflections on the water.

First projects

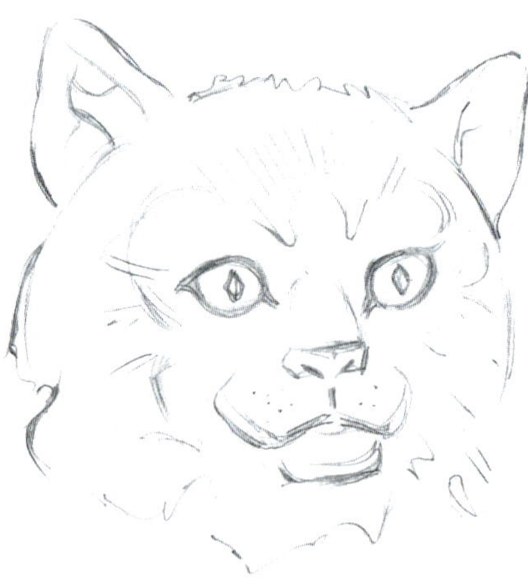

Sketch the cat's head, pressing lightly with the pencil. Remember that the more details you include, the easier it will be to colour.

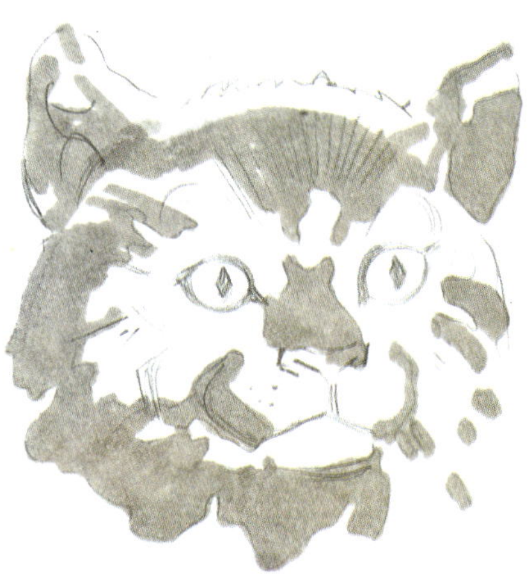

First apply a general tone, using the sketch marks as a guide. Use a round-tipped pen for the eyes, nose and mouth.

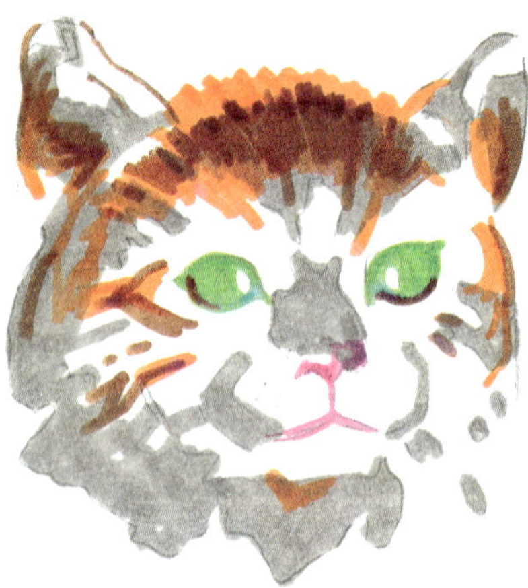

Add a lighter tone of the same colour and then blend them both together.

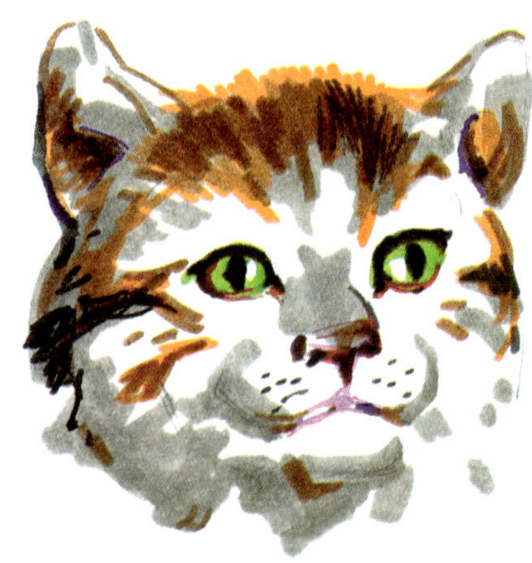

Finally, strengthen some of the lines - the eyes, the bottom of the nose and some of the markings - with a round-tipped pen.

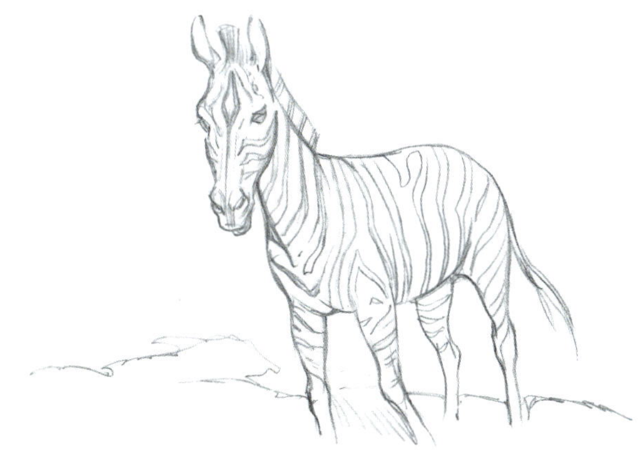

Draw the zebra, copying the picture above. Draw in the details of the face and the stripes.

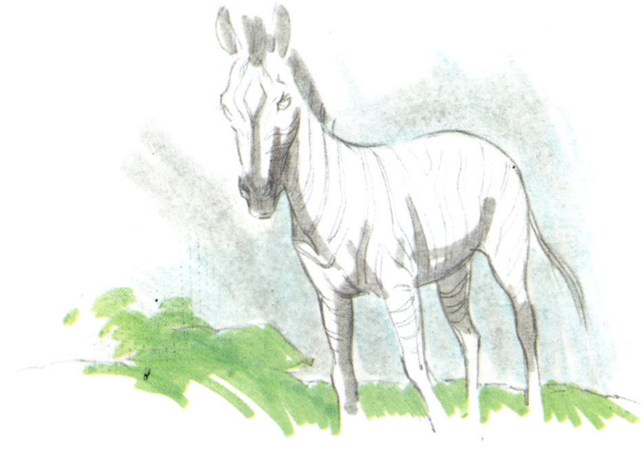

Hold a round-tipped pen at an angle and colour the shadows on the head, the side of the zebra and the ground.

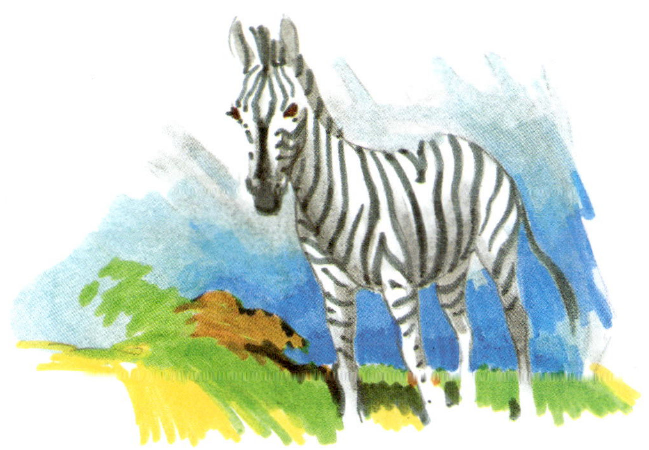

Now put in the stripes, moving the pen vertically. Then colour in the background, blending each colour with the previous one.

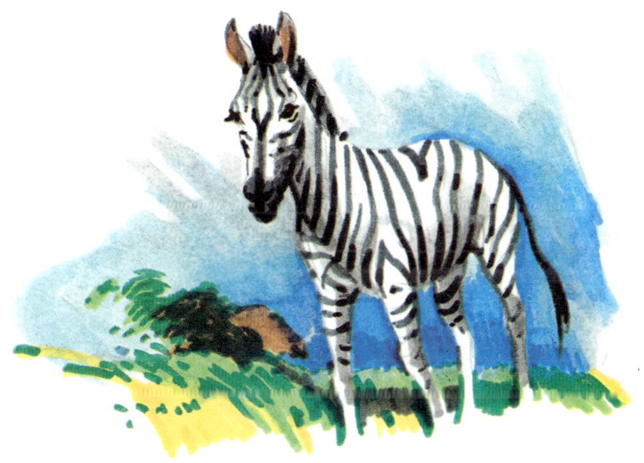

Finally, work on the darkest tones, gradating and blending the tones with lighter ones.

First projects

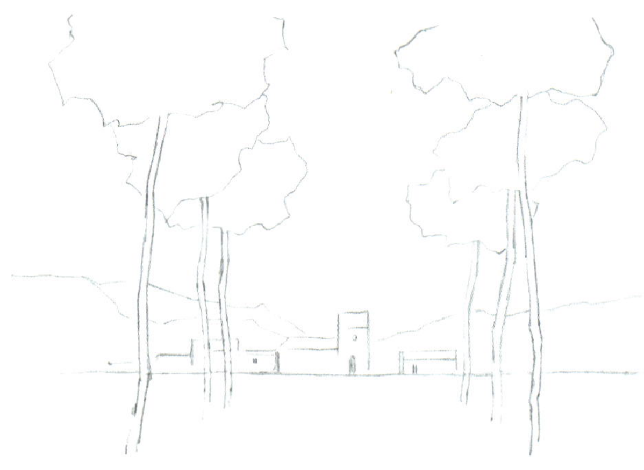

This simple landscape will help you to practise leaving visible lines without mixing colours. First sketch the scene, including as much detail as possible.

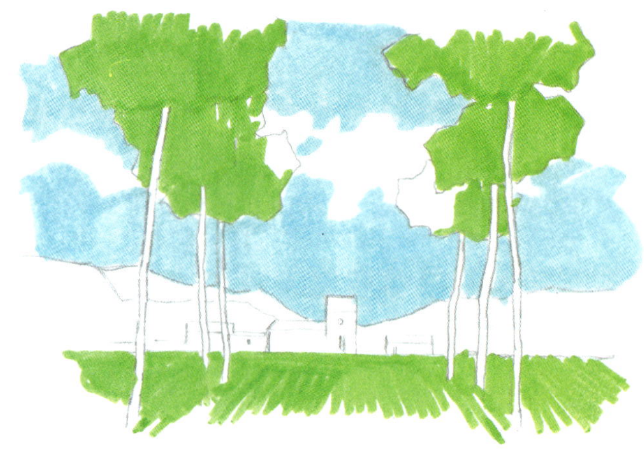

Start adding colour, holding the pen so the tip is flat, and draw lines going in the same direction.

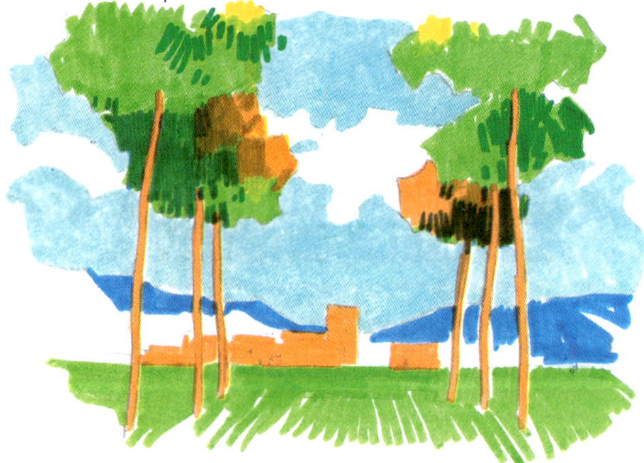

Now concentrate on the darker tones of the mountains, paint parallel lines into the tree tops, and strengthen the lines on the ground.

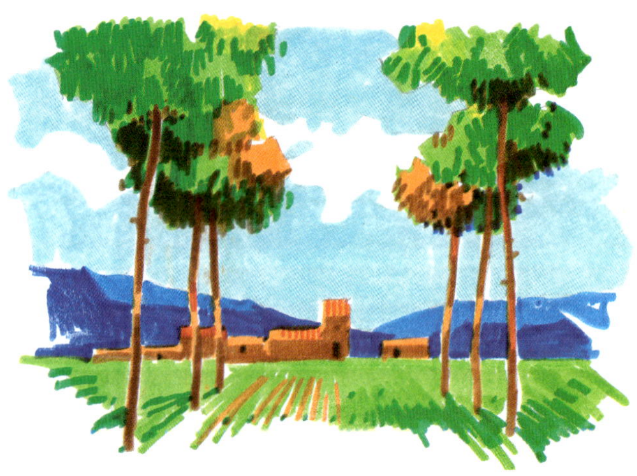

Finally, continue using parallel lines to darken the shadow tones further.

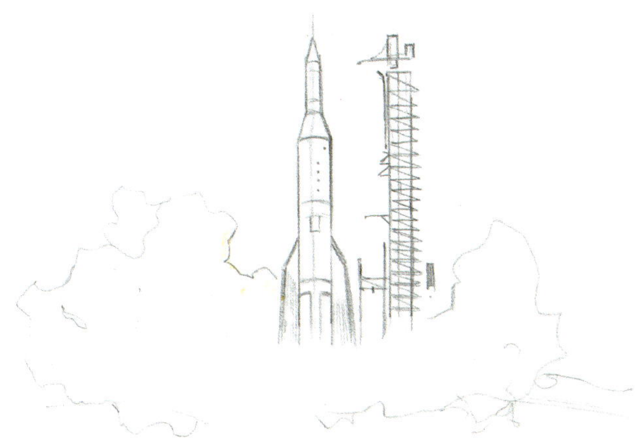

This space rocket will look spectacular when you have finished it. Draw in all the details before starting to colour.

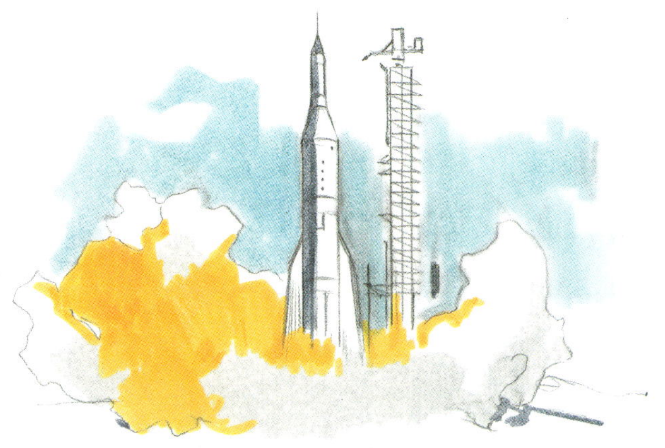

Start with a light tone, holding the pen so the tip is flat, then use a darker tone on one of the sides of the rocket.

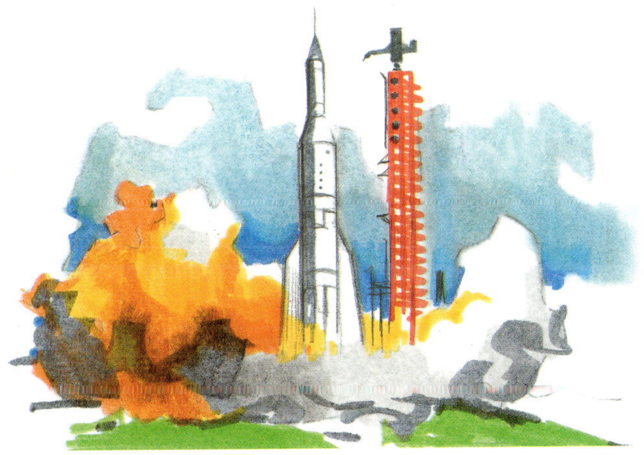

Now you can practise blending. Work on each colour separately, pressing harder with the lighter tones.

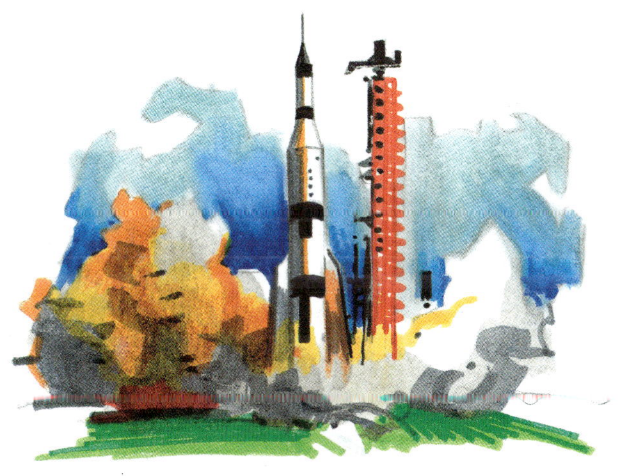

To finish the picture, work on the darker tones and continue to blend and gradate the lighter tones.

Advanced projects

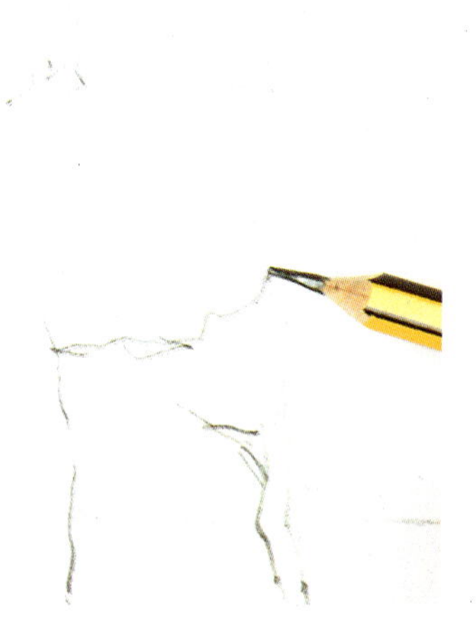

Always remember to outline the shapes within the picture carefully. This will give you a good guide when you start colouring.

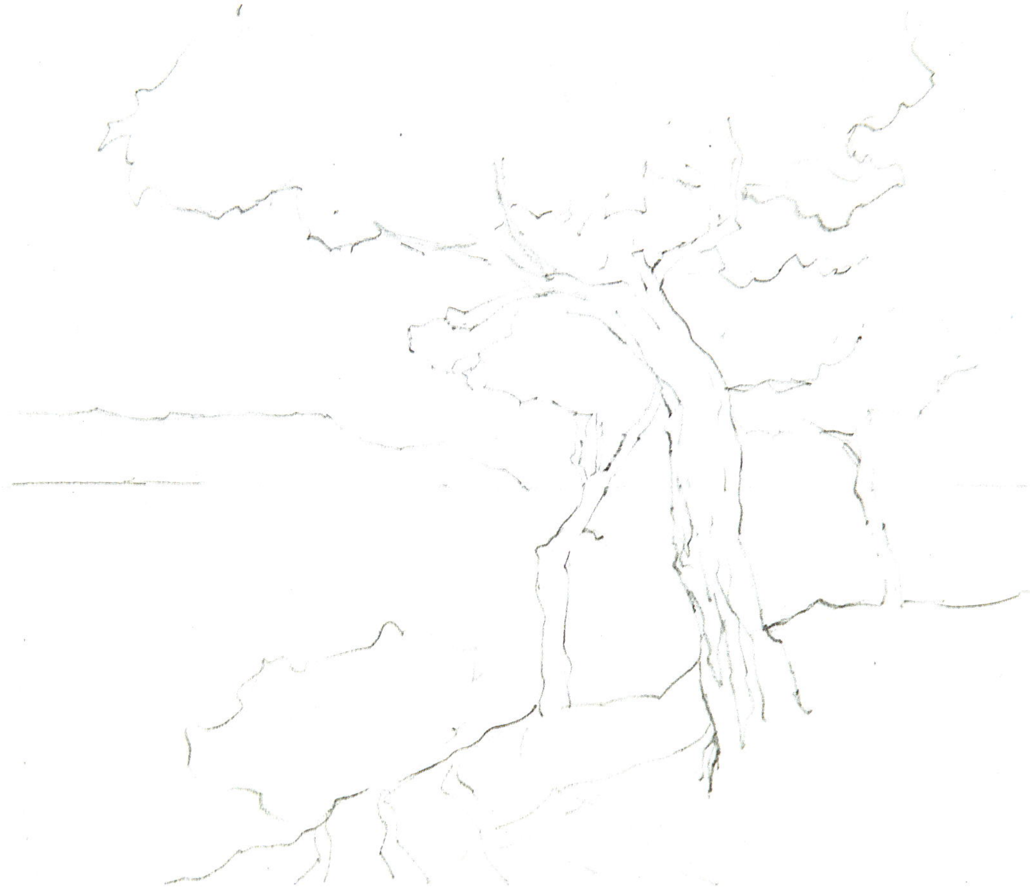

On the next few pages, there are several projects which will help you to practise everything you have learned about drawing with markers.

Follow the instructions carefully, using the colours and techniques suggested for each step.

The first project uses the visible line technique.

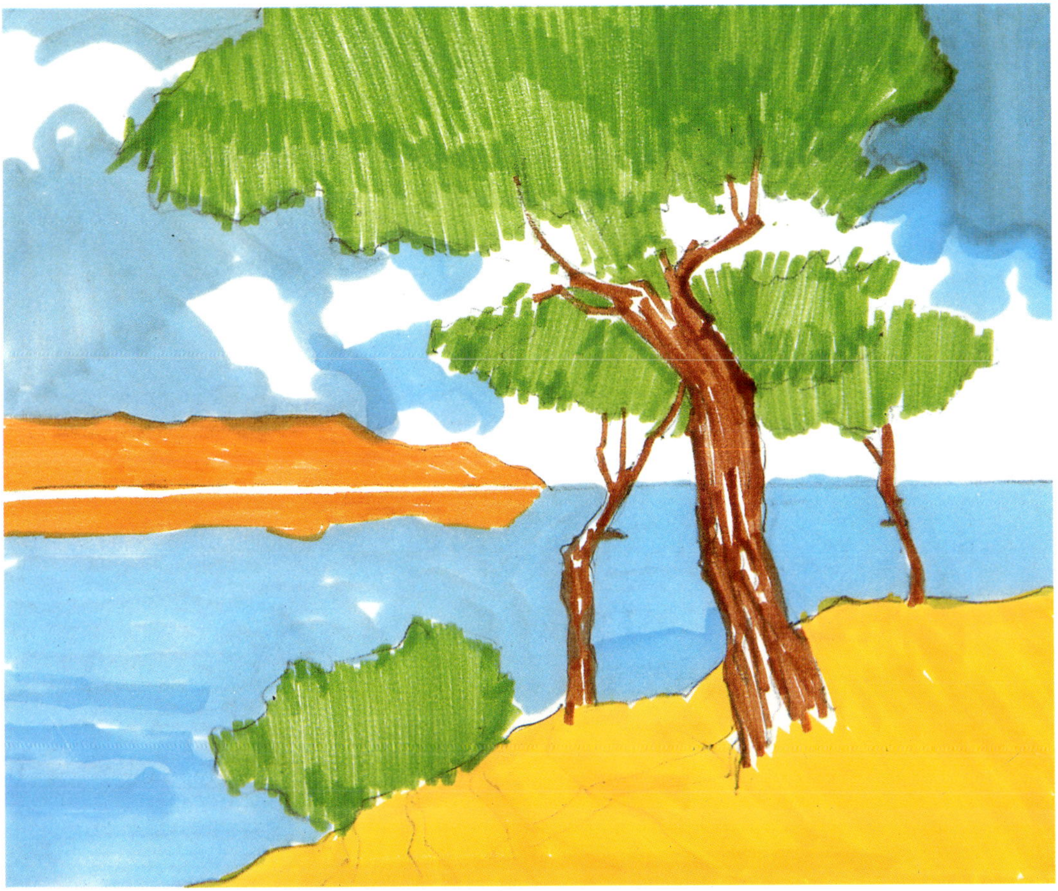

Advanced projects

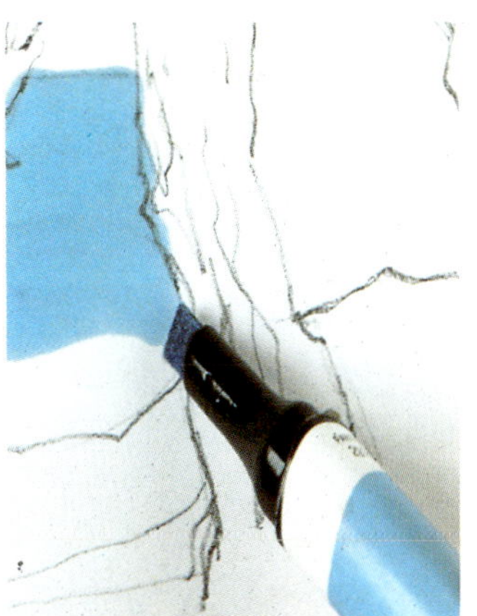

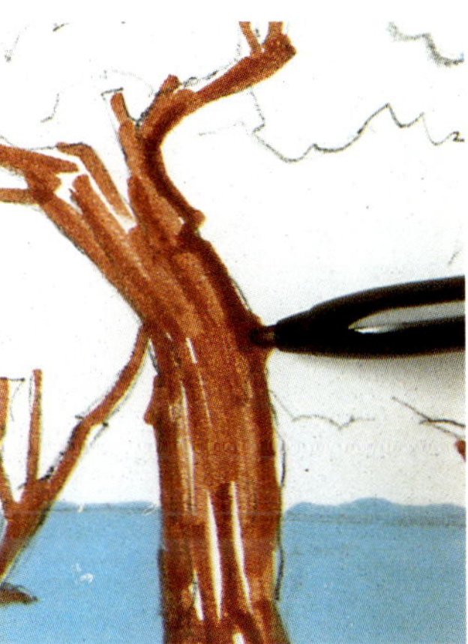

Start with the background and large surfaces. Use the flat end of the tip of a flat-tipped pen to colour the clouds, the horizon, the sea, and the small hill in the foreground.

Always move the pen in the same direction, using the same amount of pressure and without stopping, to avoid colouring unevenly. Next colour the tree tops and trunks with a round-tipped felt pen.

Advanced projects

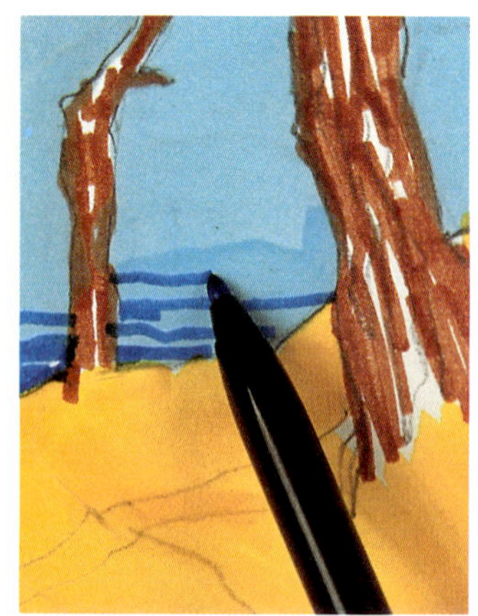

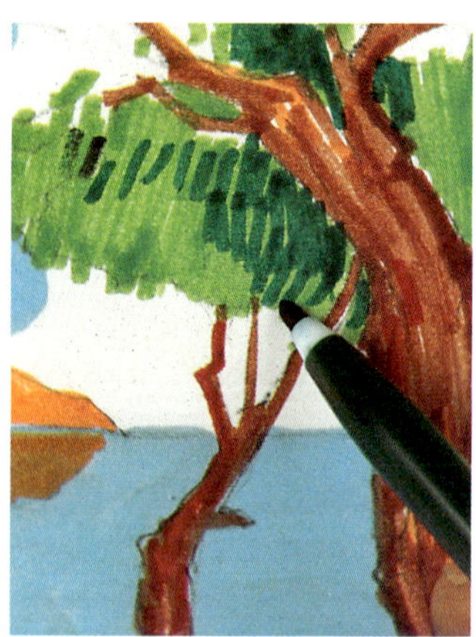

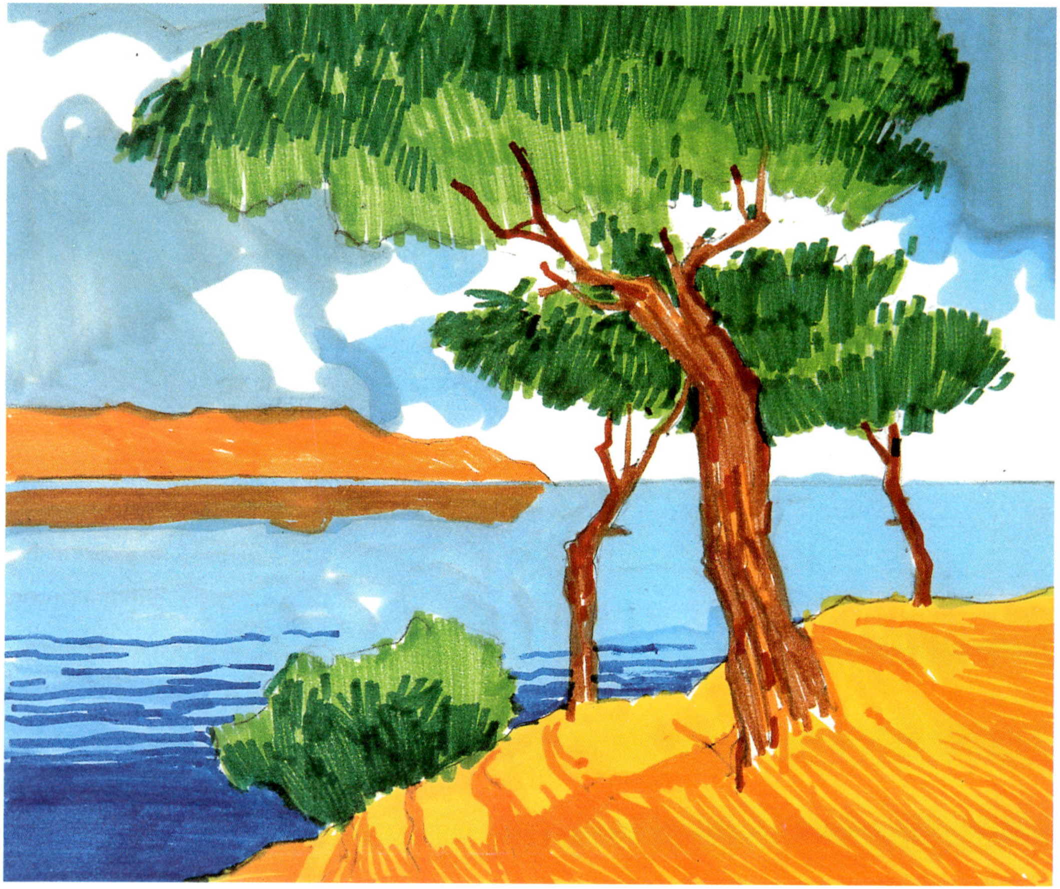

Continue working on the tones.

Colour in the sea in the bottom left-hand corner and draw in lines, each one a bit more widely spaced than the last.

Do the same with the small hill in the foreground, to show the shadows of the trees. Finally, colour in the tree tops and the trunks. Add some darker lines between the ones you have already drawn.

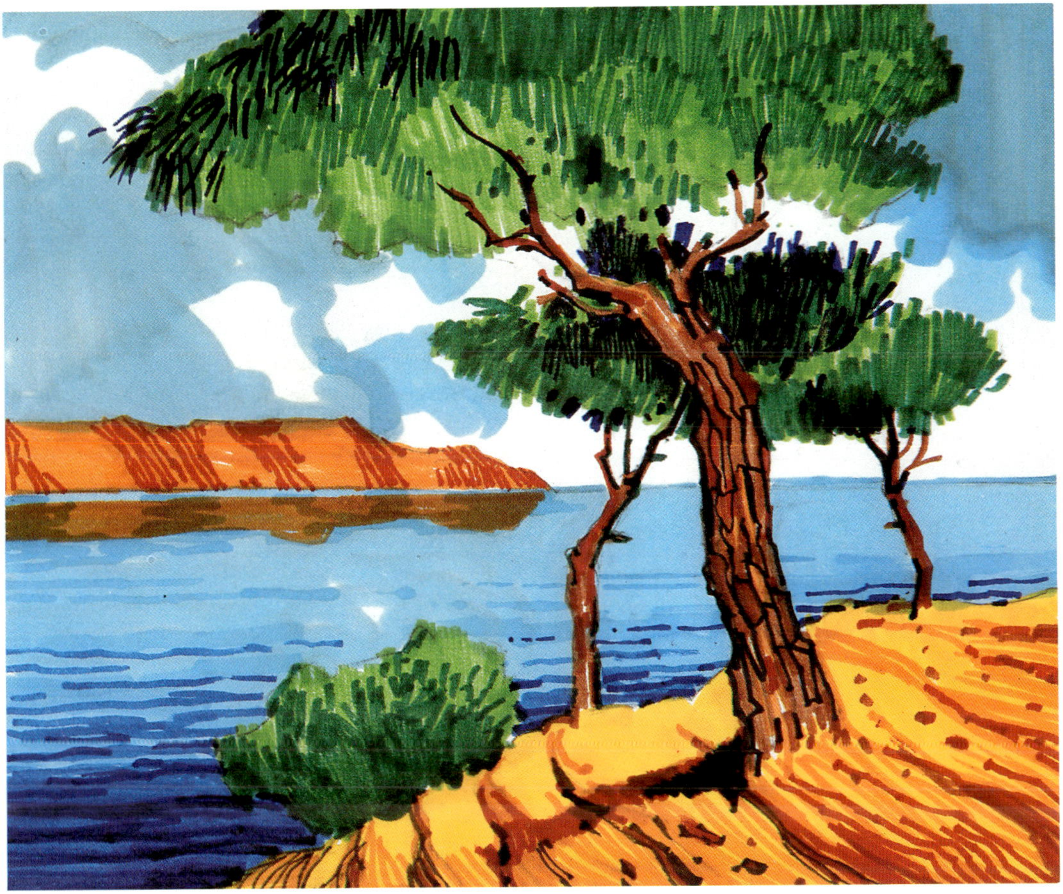

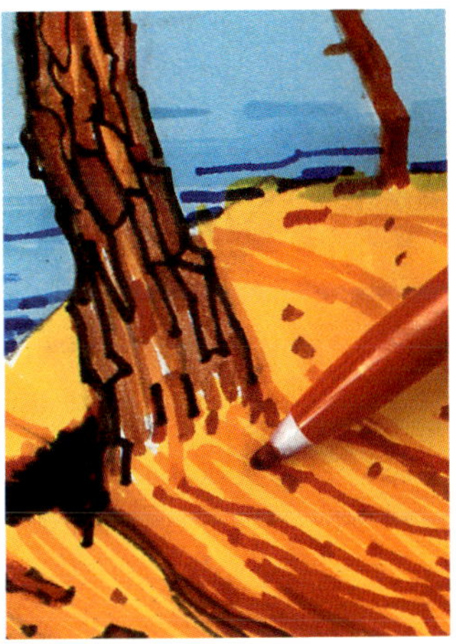

This picture is a good example of how the parallel line technique is used: the lines are painted with different tones.

The final touches depend on you.

You do not need to copy every line on the picture above, but can decide for yourself what you would like to put in and what to leave out in order to achieve your final result.

You can also try experimenting with different colours, and different kinds of markers.

Advanced projects

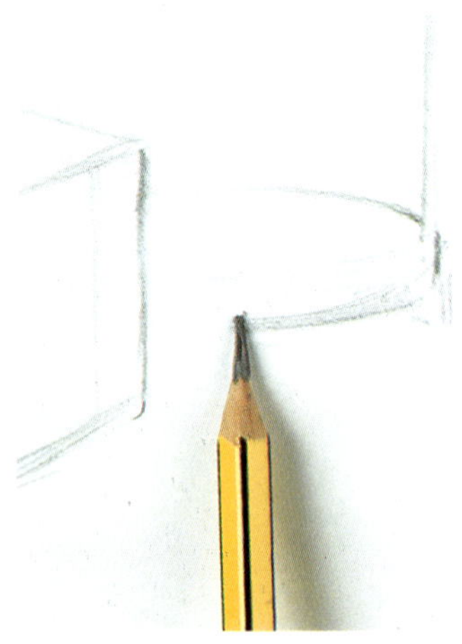

Sketch a complete circle to represent the bottom of the pot holding the markers.

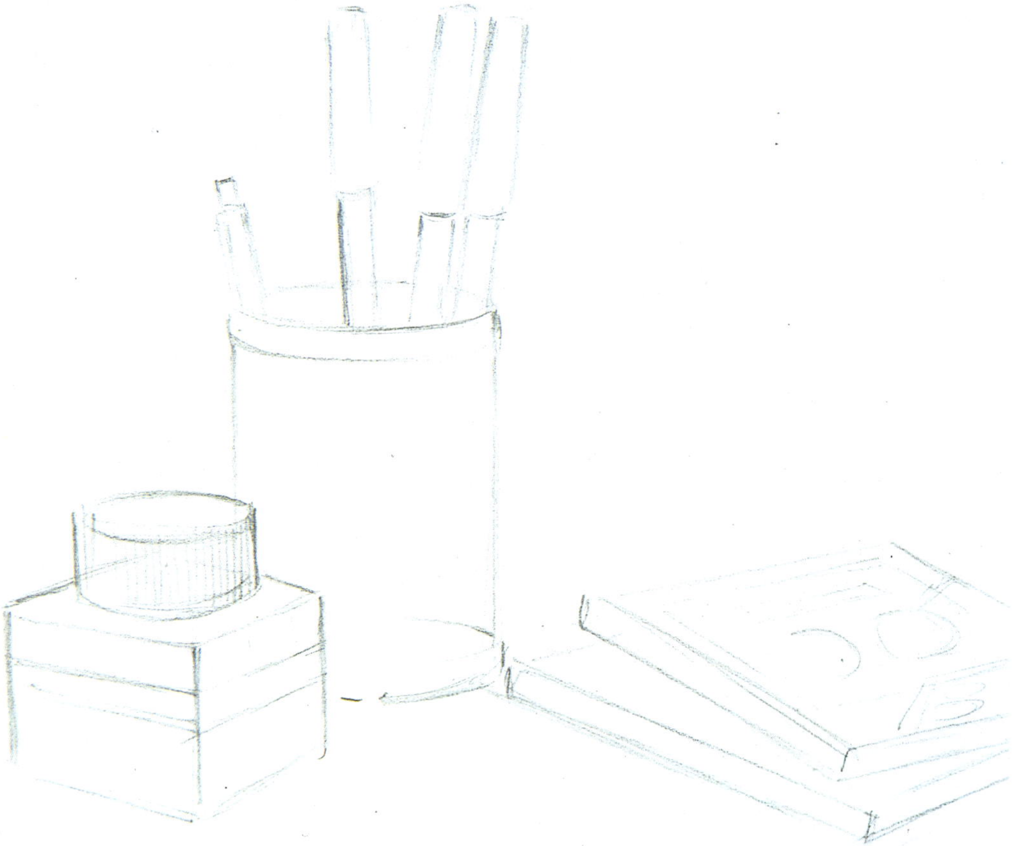

A good drawing is half the work of the completed picture. The next project is to paint the simple still-life shown here.

Use a hard or semi-hard pencil, trying not to rub out too much. If you draw with very heavy pencil lines, the ink of the pen will not cover them when you colour over the top.

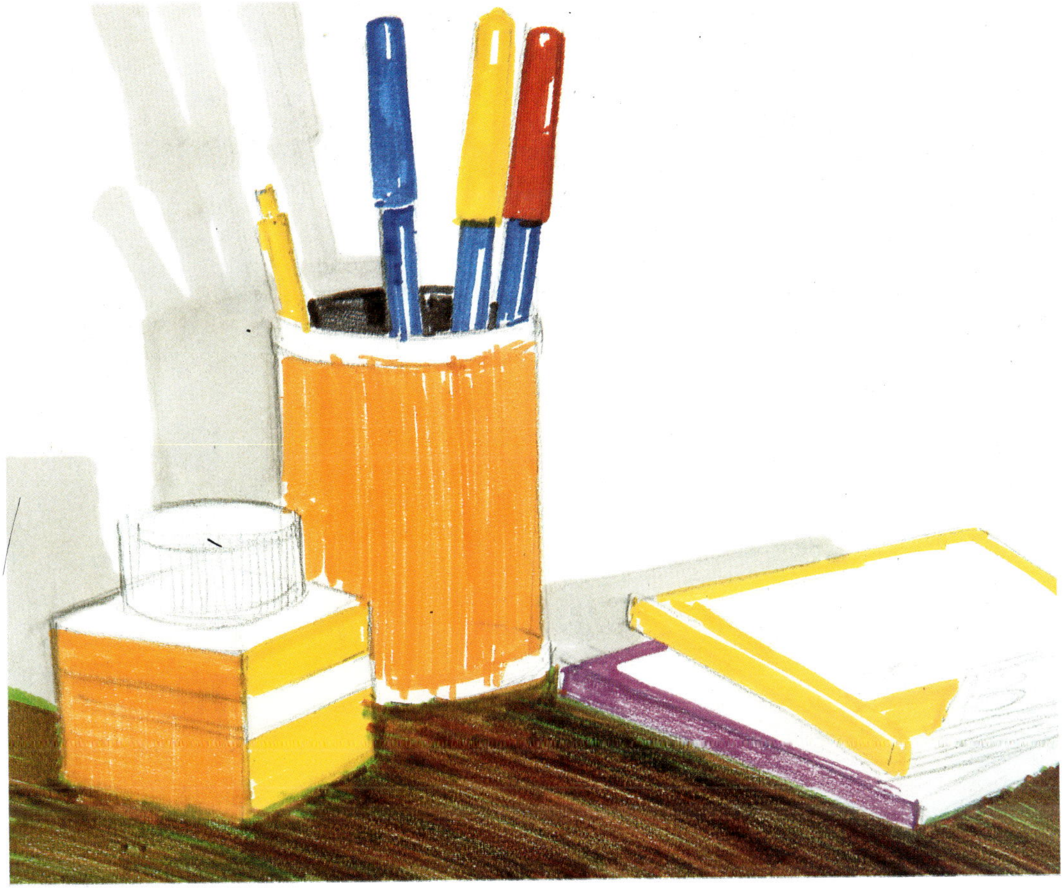

Advanced projects

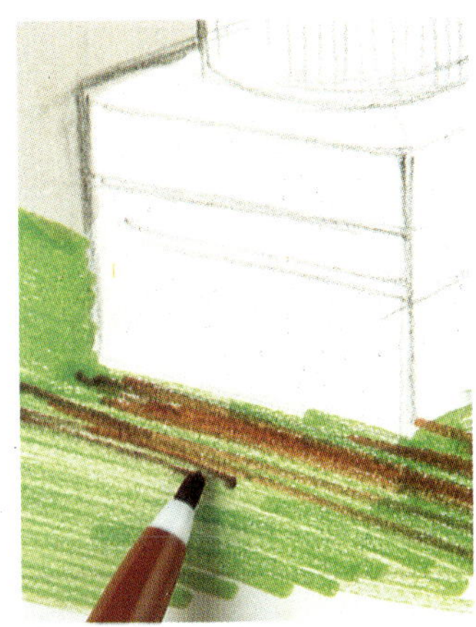

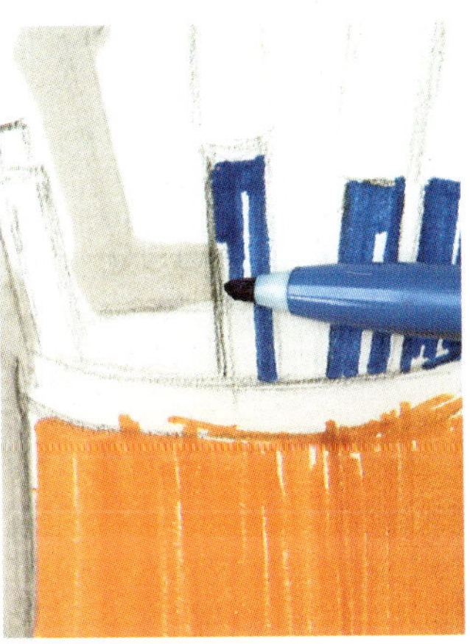

Start with the background. Colour with light green, drawing the lines in the same direction. Then colour the shadows of the ink bottle, the pot and books with grey.

Now colour in each object, outlining them first.

Then do a simple colour mix: brown on top of the green background you coloured first.

Advanced projects

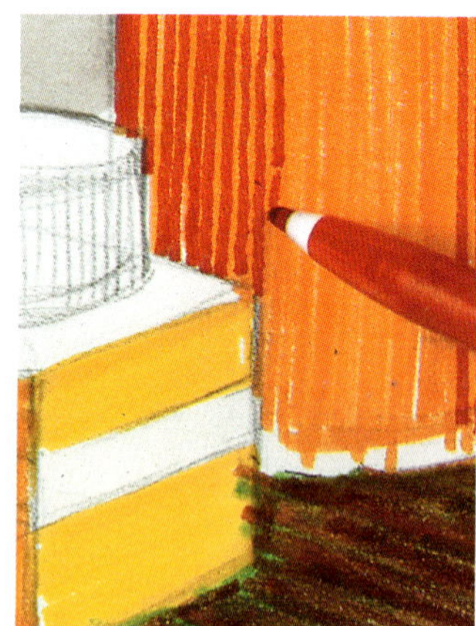

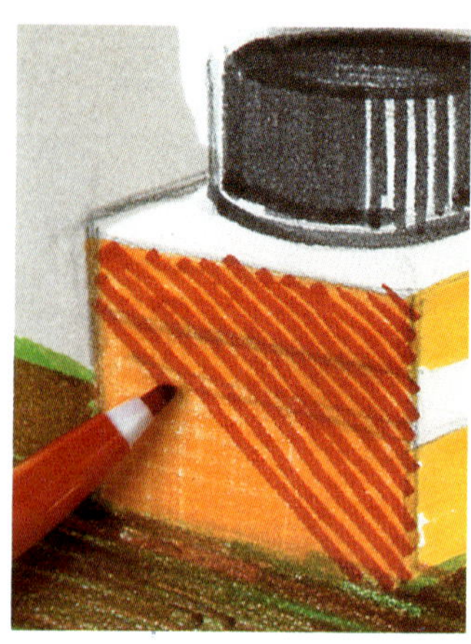

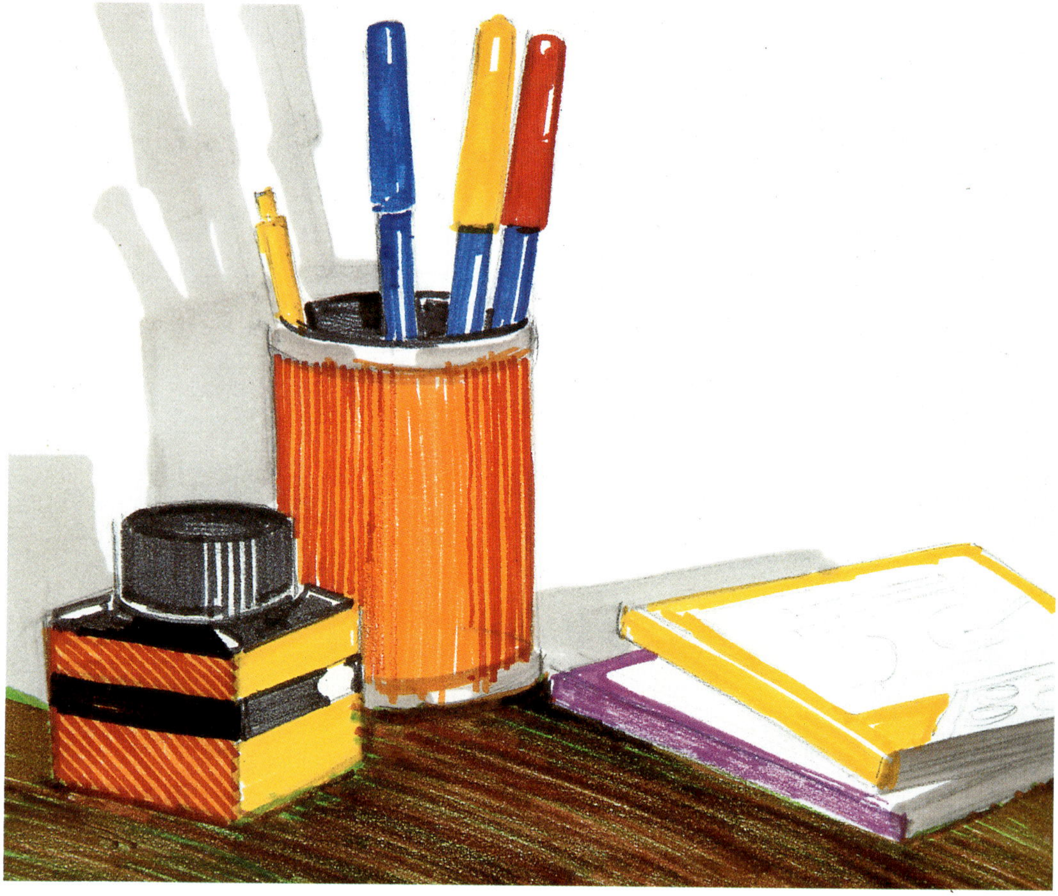

Continue adding to the earlier colours. Make sure that you draw the lines of the pot and ink bottle in the same direction.

Finish off the ink bottle with a black pen.

Then add soft strokes of grey to the sides of the books.

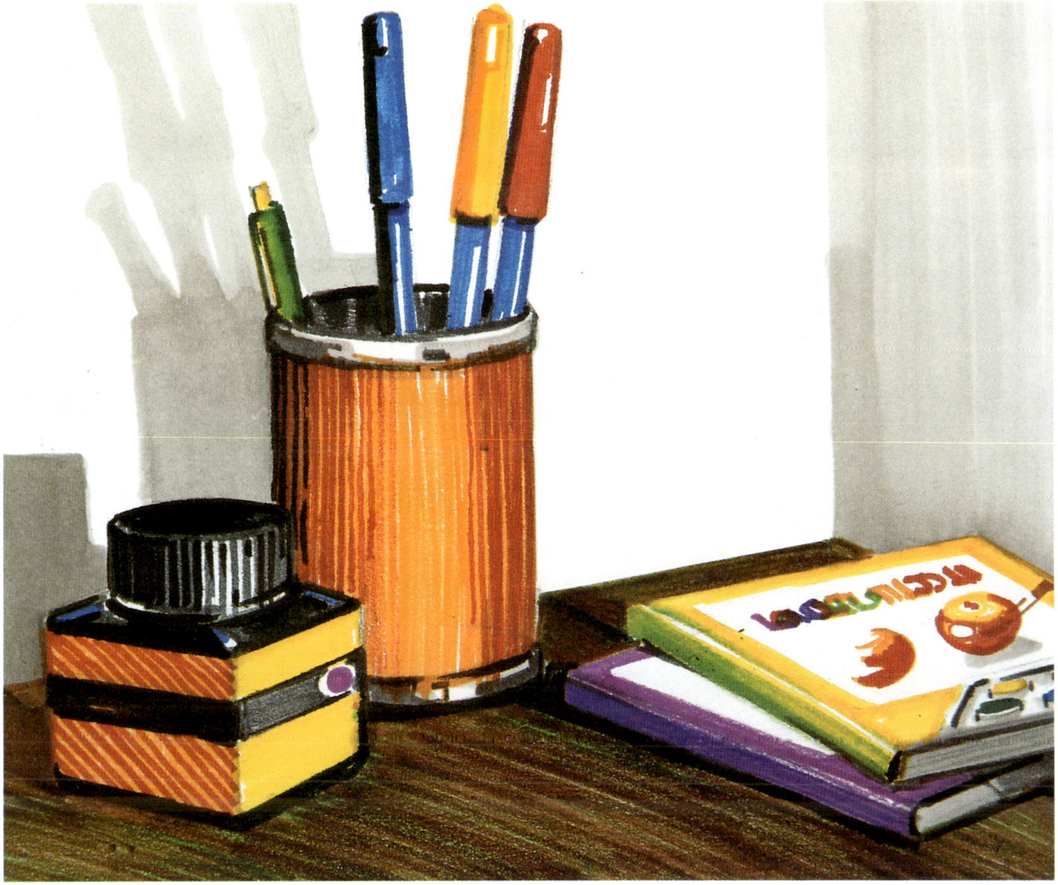

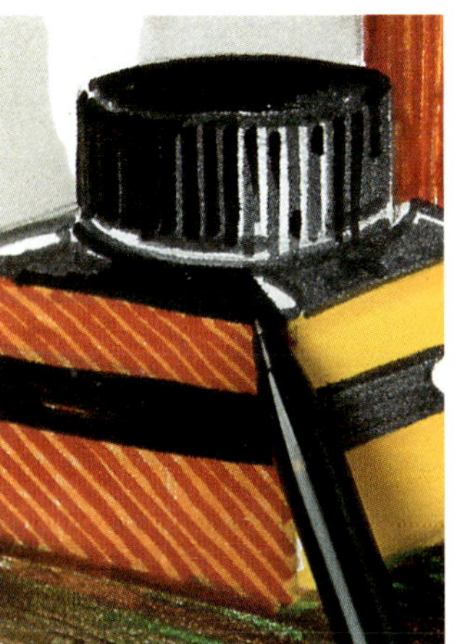

You can create a more intense black on the left-hand side of the picture and on top of the ink bottle by pressing down harder on the pen.

Now you need to strengthen some of the lines, using mostly the black pen. Use a round-tipped grey pen to darken the shadows of the pot and the ink bottle, and colour the rest of the background in the top right-hand corner. Finally, add some green and violet to the spines of the books, and do a rough impression of the title and illustration on the cover of the top one.

Advanced projects

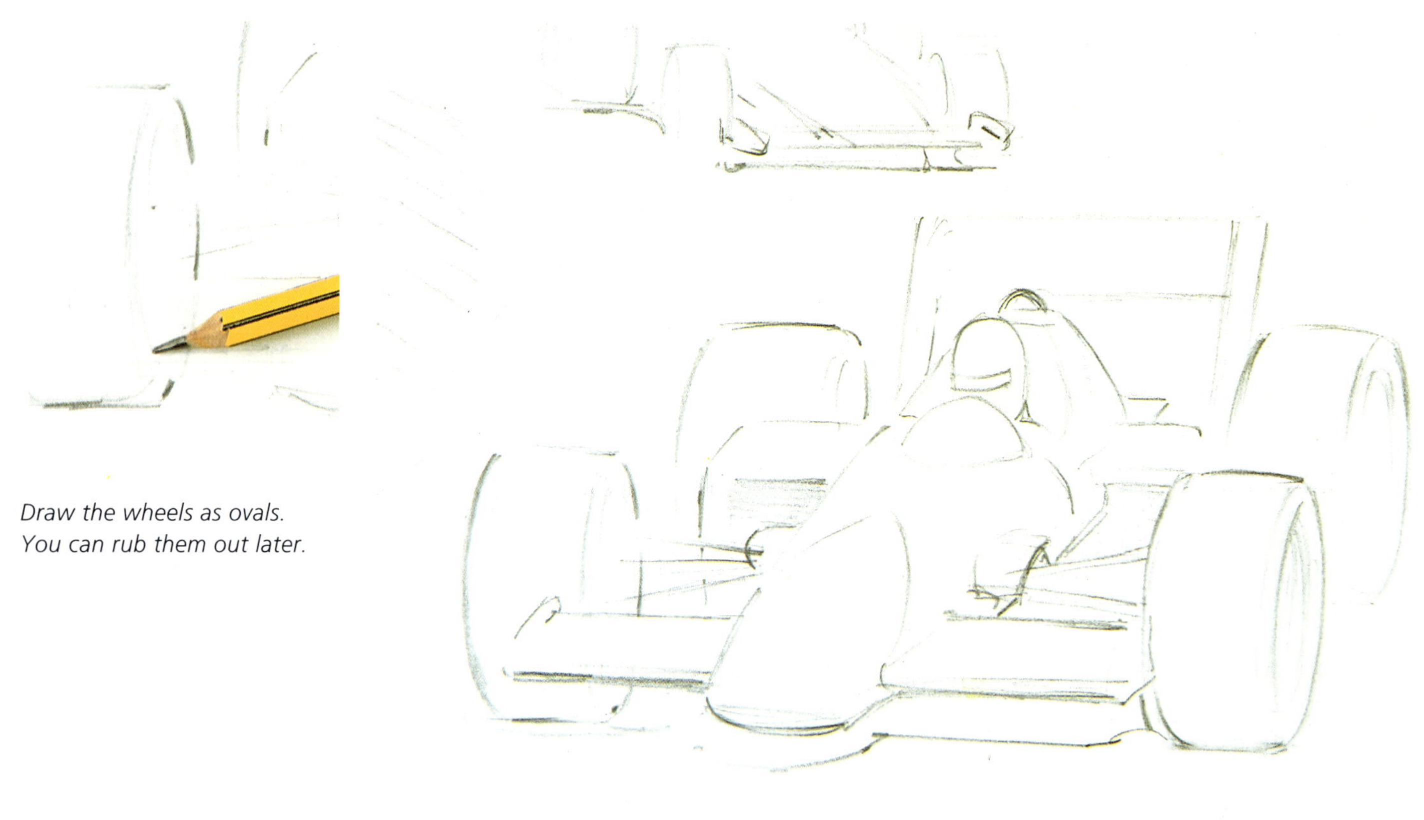

Draw the wheels as ovals. You can rub them out later.

Copy the car as closely as possible. It's easier than it looks!

Box in the basic shapes of the picture, including the bodies of the two cars (especially the one in the foreground), the spoilers and the wheels. This should help you to get the proportions right. Once you have boxed in the basic outlines, you will find it easier to draw in the details.

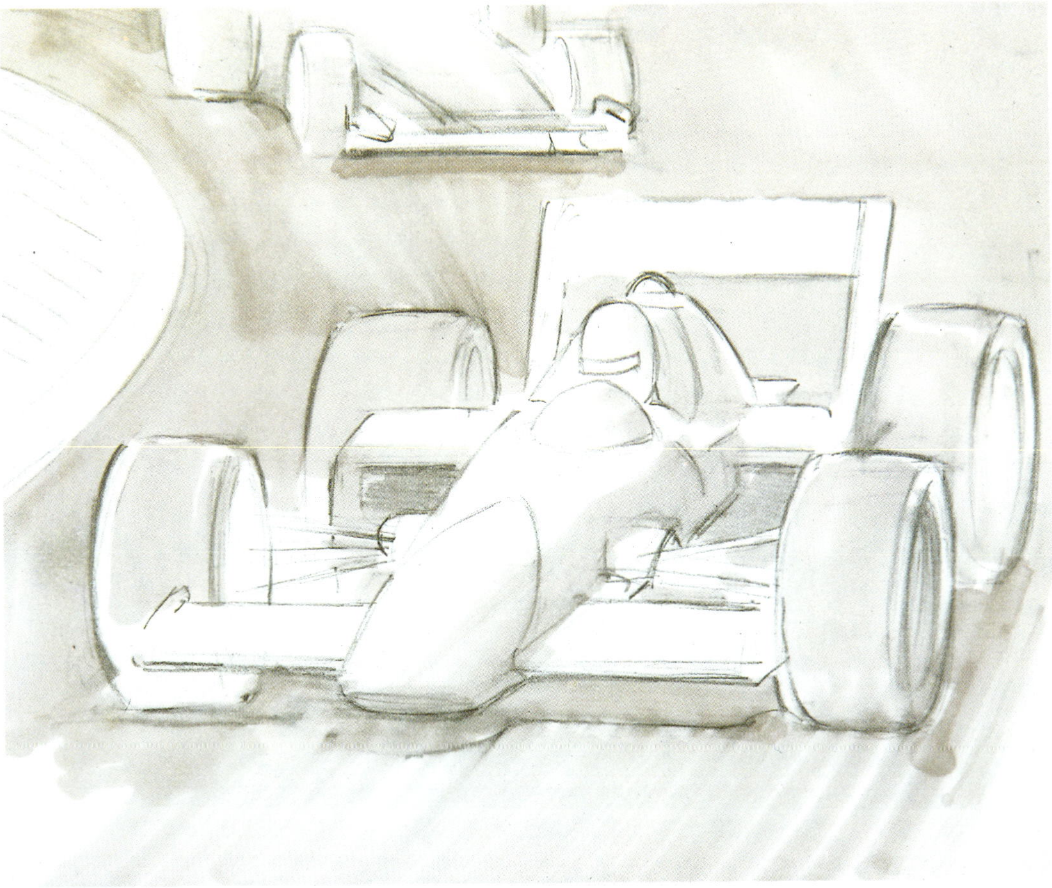

Advanced projects

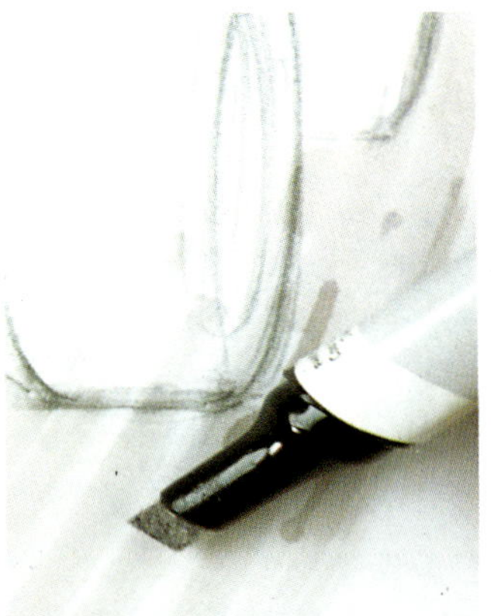

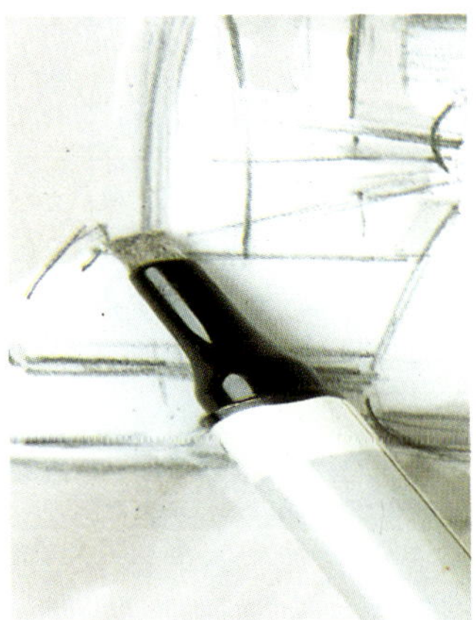

Now you can practise colouring in a large background. Remember to make sure that you colour evenly, so that you don't leave more ink in some areas than others.

Use a flat-tipped pen, holding it parallel to the paper, to colour wide areas. Use only the edge of the tip to outline the shapes.

Advanced projects

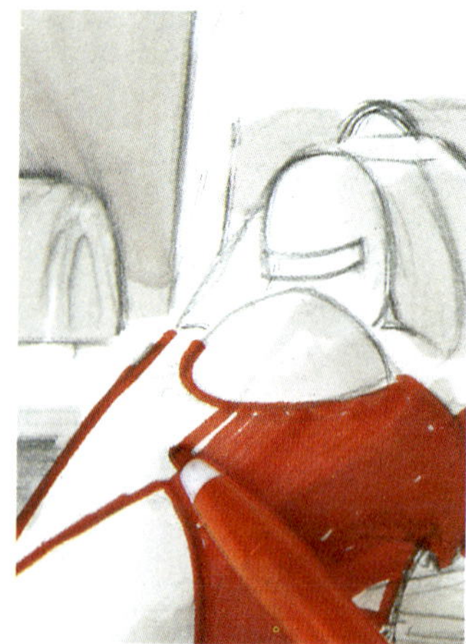

First outline the shape, then colour it in

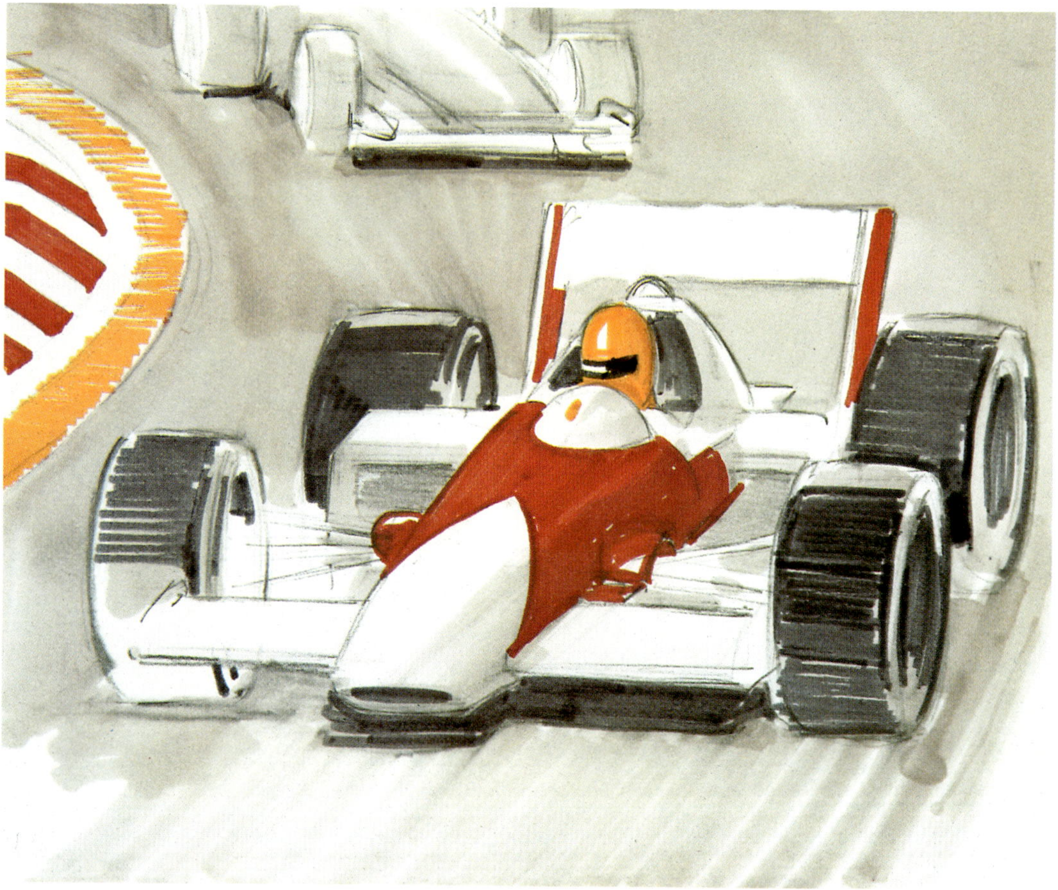

Now use a round-tipped pen to paint the car bodies and the strip of pavement.

Colour the pavement as a semi-circle, drawing the lines gradually further apart.

Finish this stage by sketching in the cars' shadows with a black pen and adding horizontal lines to the wheels.

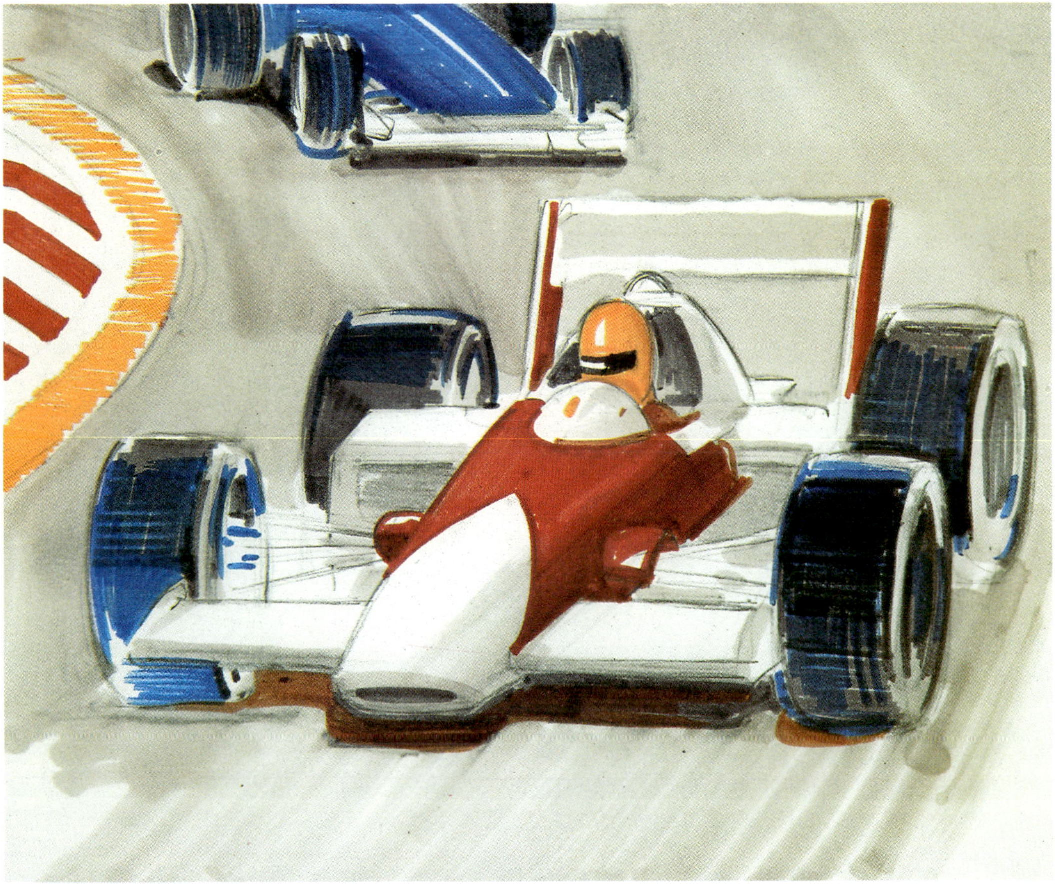

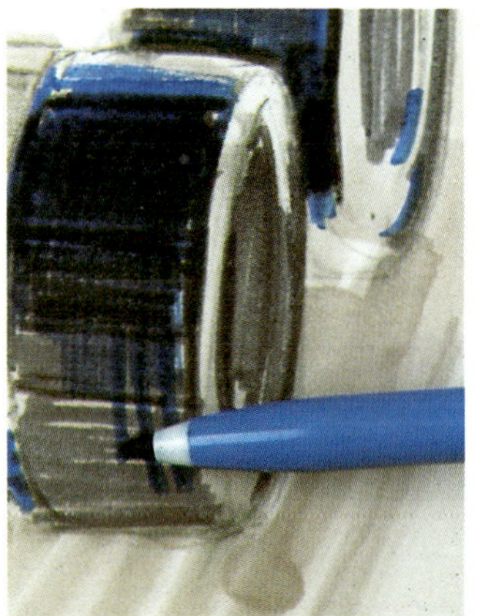

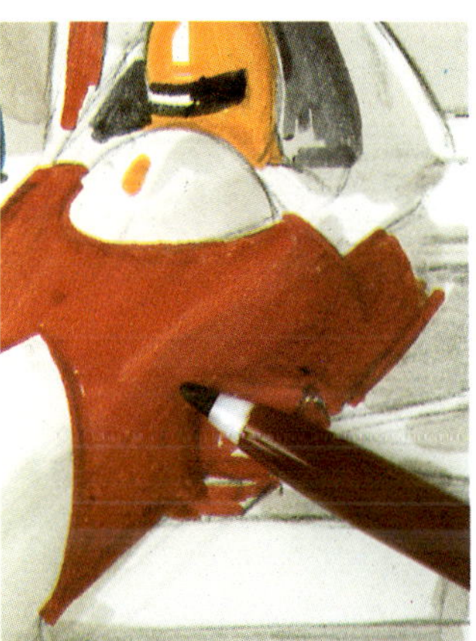

Now it's time to add more colours in the same way as before.

Put some red on to the shadows of the car in the foreground. Use blue for the other car's bodywork, and then add vertical lines with a light blue round-tipped pen to the wheels.

Advanced projects

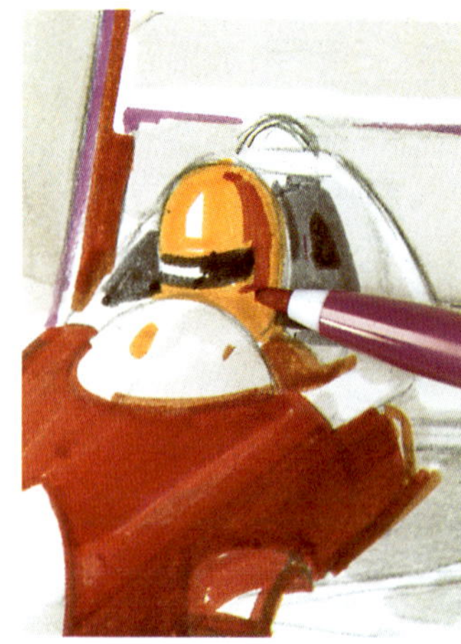

This is an area where the colours should not be mixed. The red line will not mix with the previous colour.

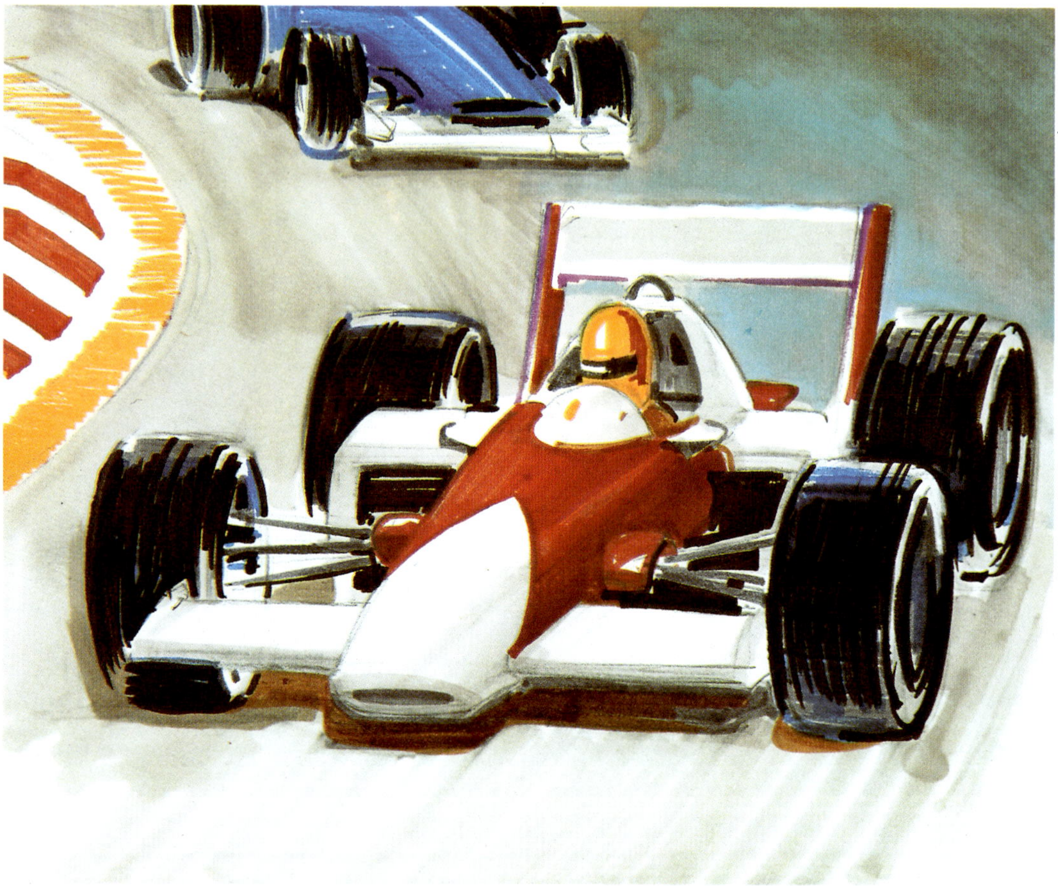

For this stage in the picture you need just two pens - black and blue.

Use a flat-tipped pen in the top right-hand section of the background for your first mixes. Press the pen firmly until you blend the colour with the one underneath.

Then draw vertical lines with the round-tipped black on the wheels and next to the bodywork.

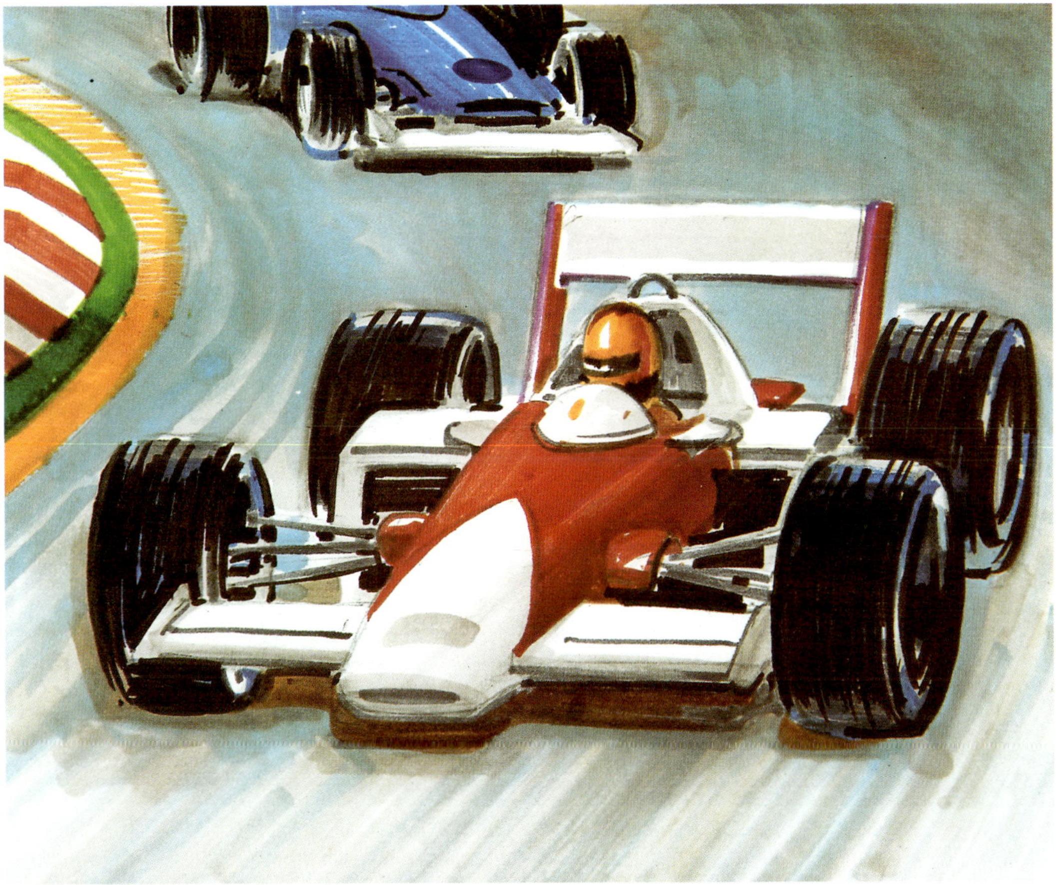

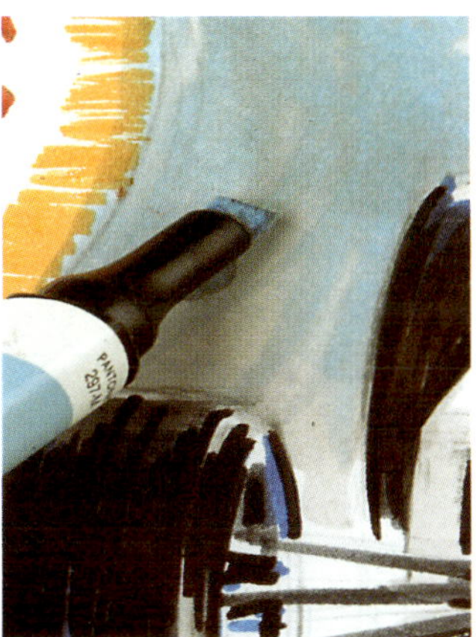

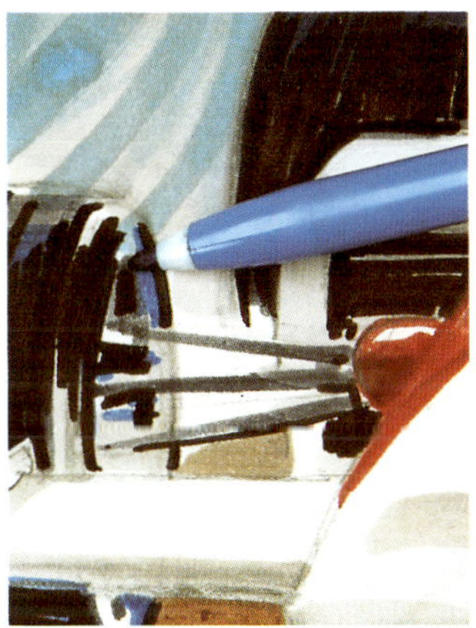

Use the flat-tipped blue pen to blend the background.

Colour a green strip on the left-hand side, putting more pressure on one side to create a darker tone.

Finally, use the round-tipped blue to paint in the white spaces between the wheels and to add some loose lines around the pavement.

Advanced projects

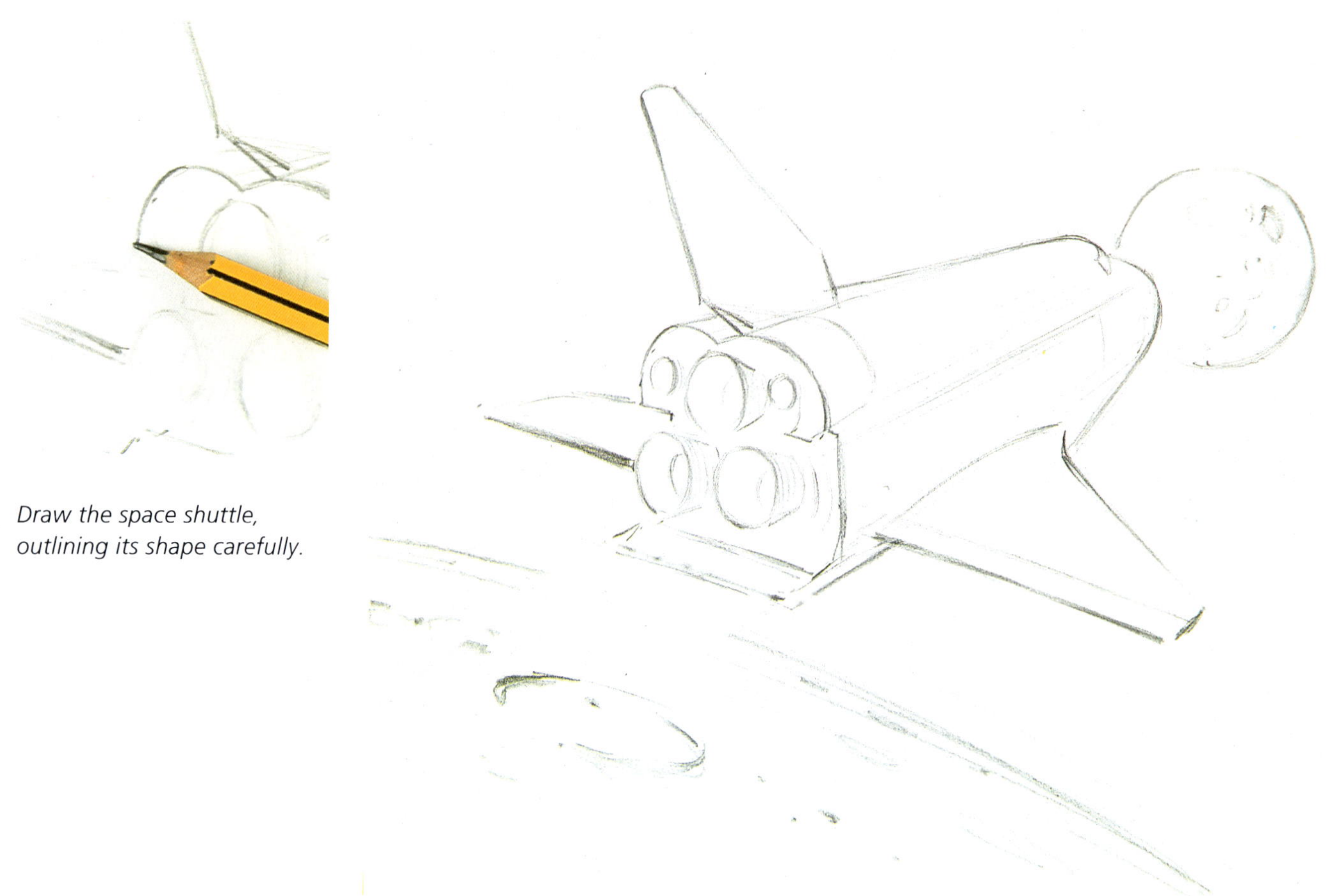

Draw the space shuttle, outlining its shape carefully.

By the time you get to this page, you should have begun to see what you can do with markers, fibre tips and felt-tipped pens.

In this project, you will be able to put all that you've learned into practice. If you have practised the techniques described earlier in the book, you will not find the picture difficult.

First sketch the picture shown above.

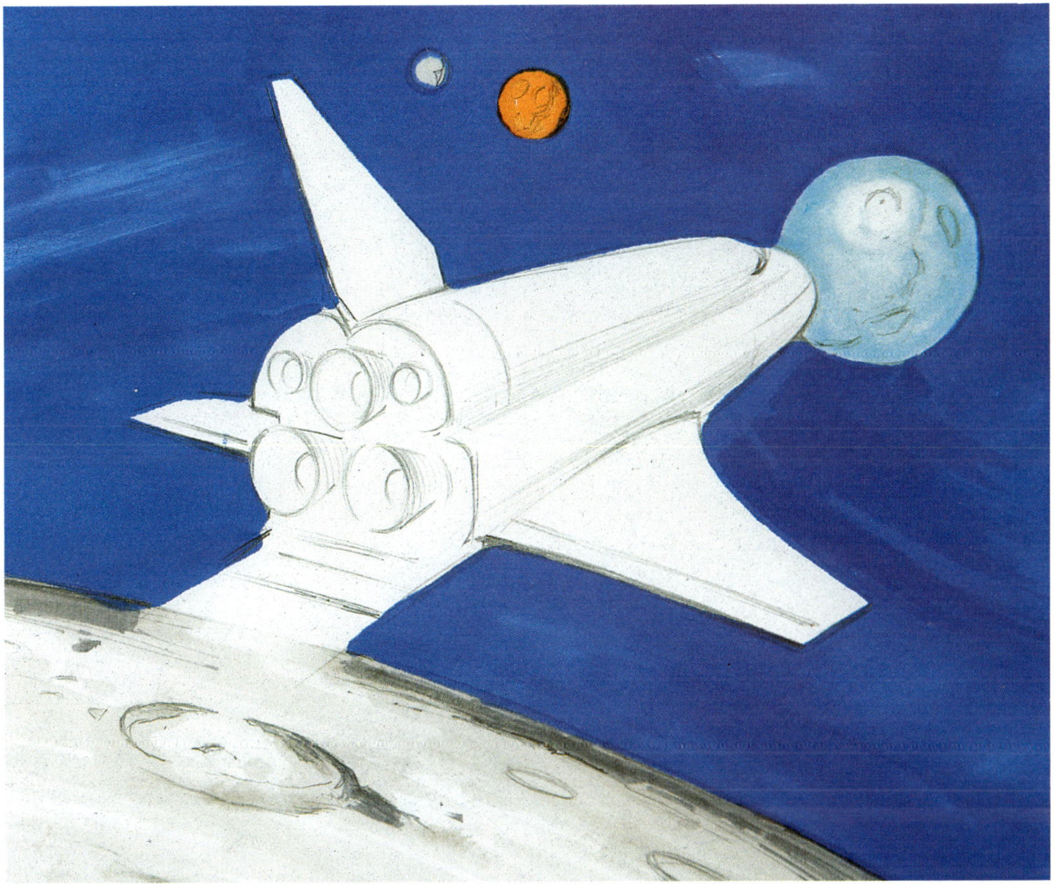

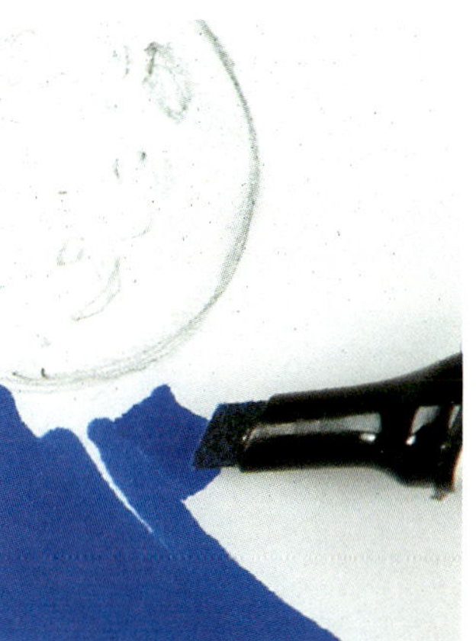

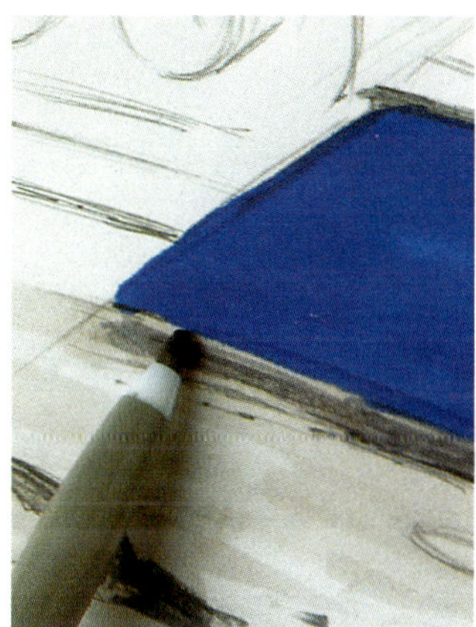

As before, start by colouring the large areas.

Colour the sky fairly quickly, being careful not to leave too much ink around the shapes of the shuttle and the planets.

Colour the planet in the foreground using a round-tipped pen.

Advanced projects

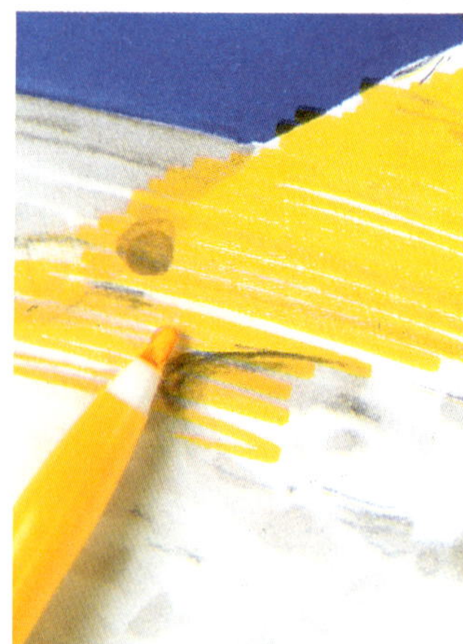

Remember that the way to prevent lines overlapping is to outline the shape and then colour it in.

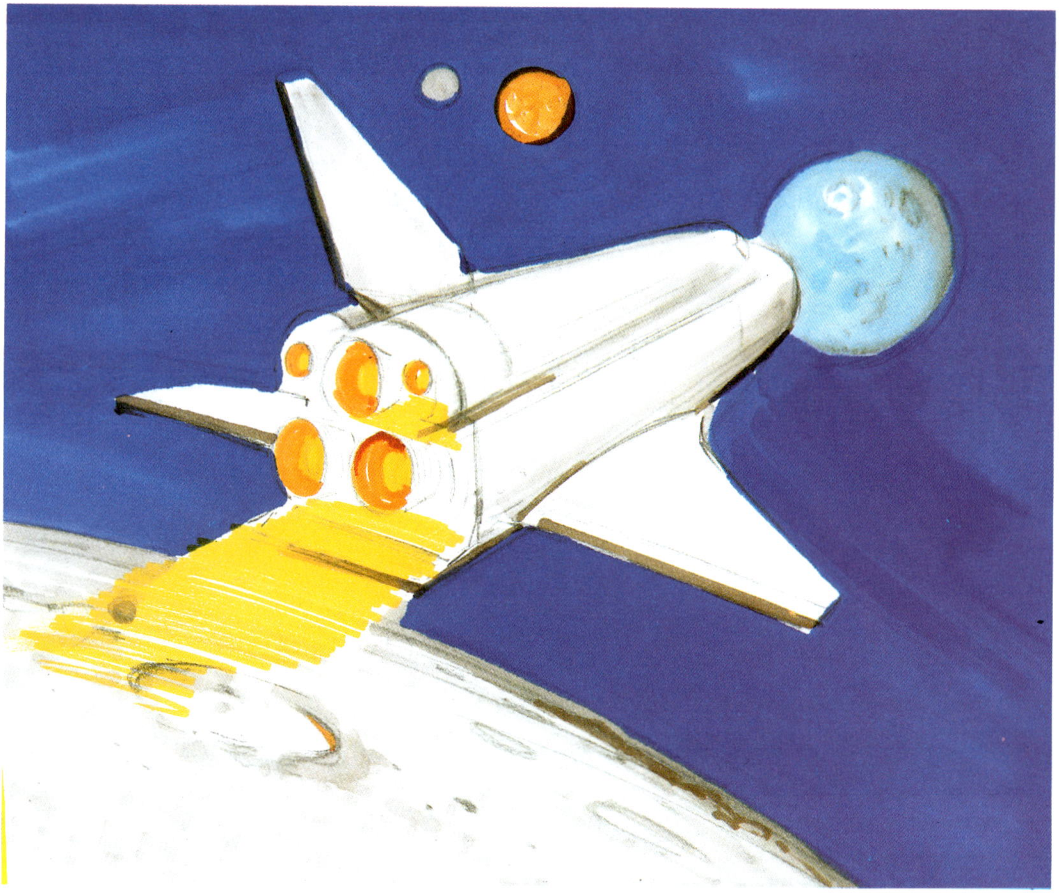

Once you have coloured in the background, you can start to add other colours.

Colour the craters of the planet in the foreground, the other planets, and the shuttle's reactors with a light tone.

Use round-tipped pens, pressing the tip into a flat position on the paper.

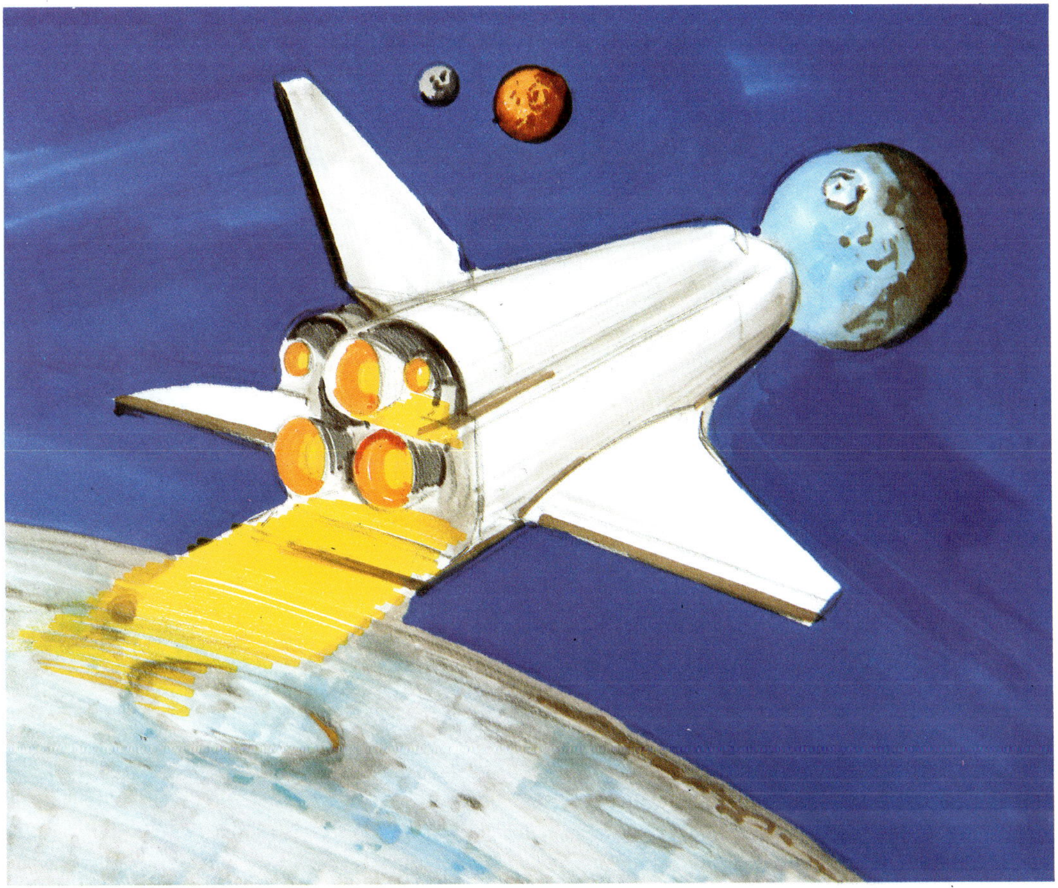

Advanced projects

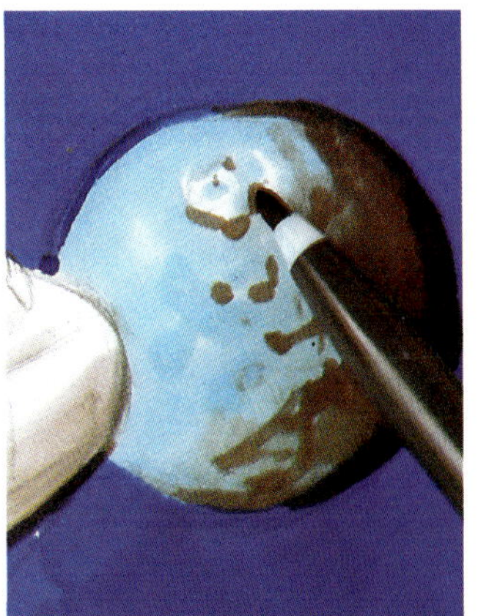

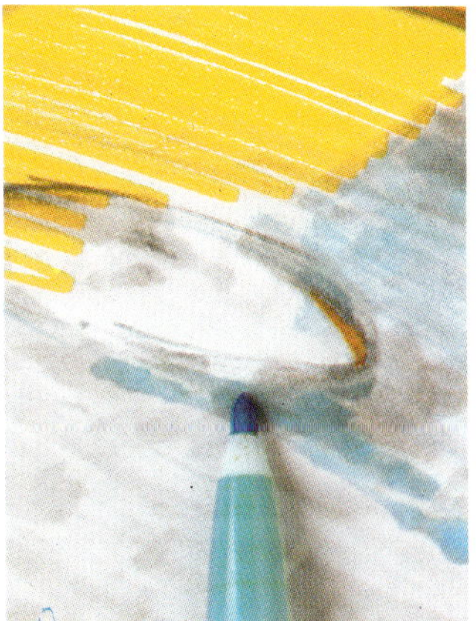

Next work on the shuttle's dark tones, strengthening the tones you've already completed.

Colour the surface of the planet in the foreground.

Use a light tone and press lightly, just as you would with a pencil.

Advanced projects

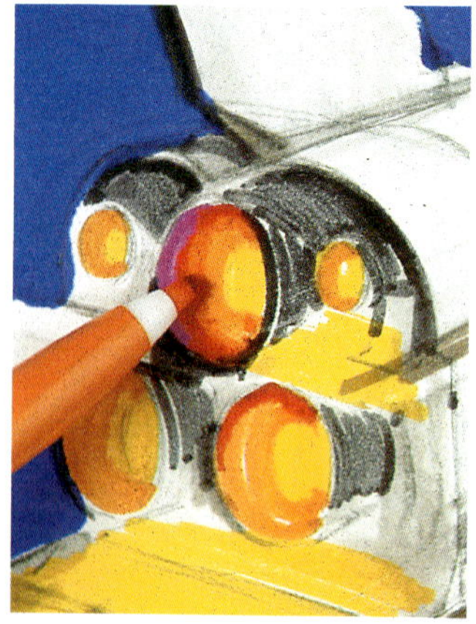

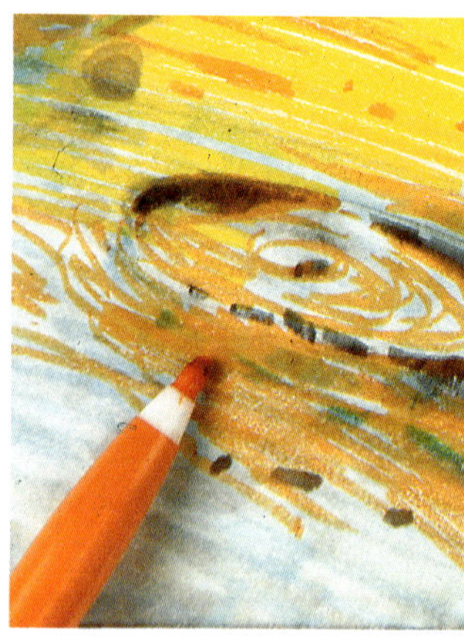

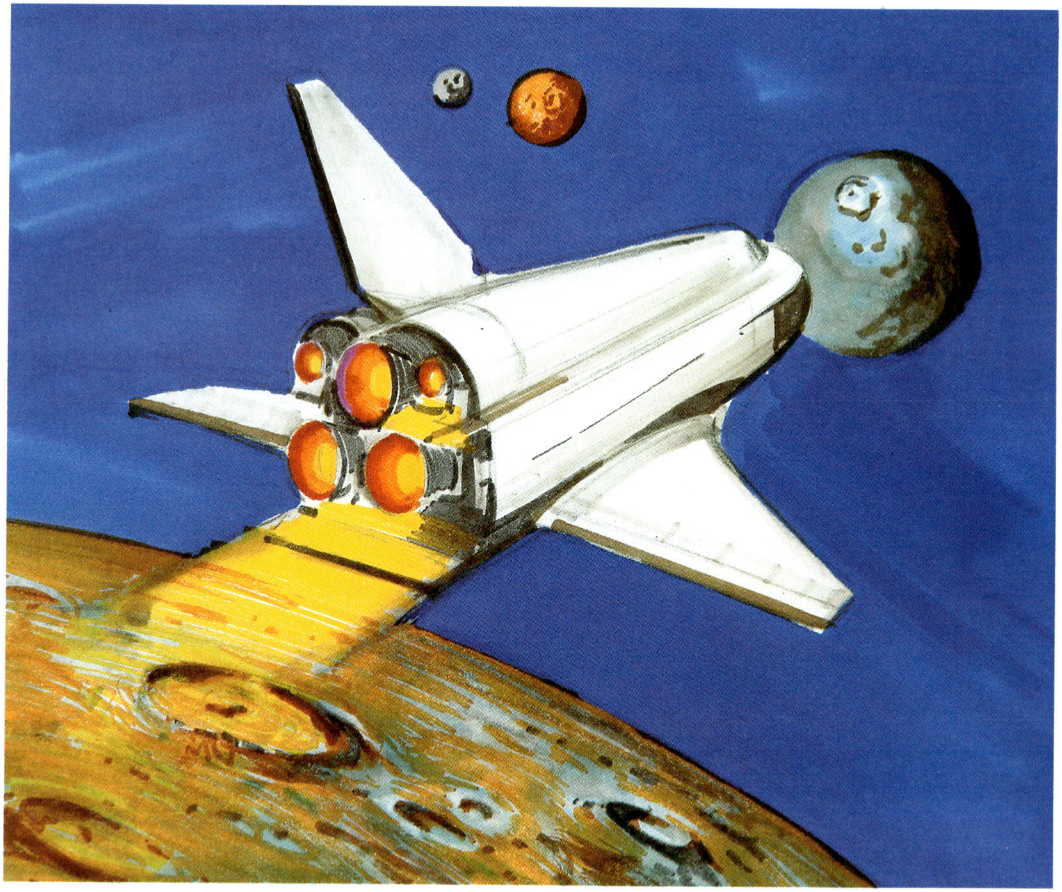

Next work on all the colours, blending them with the ones underneath.

Use heavier pressure with the light tones so that they blend well, especially in the shuttle's reactor.

Work on the shadows on the asteroid in front of the shuttle.

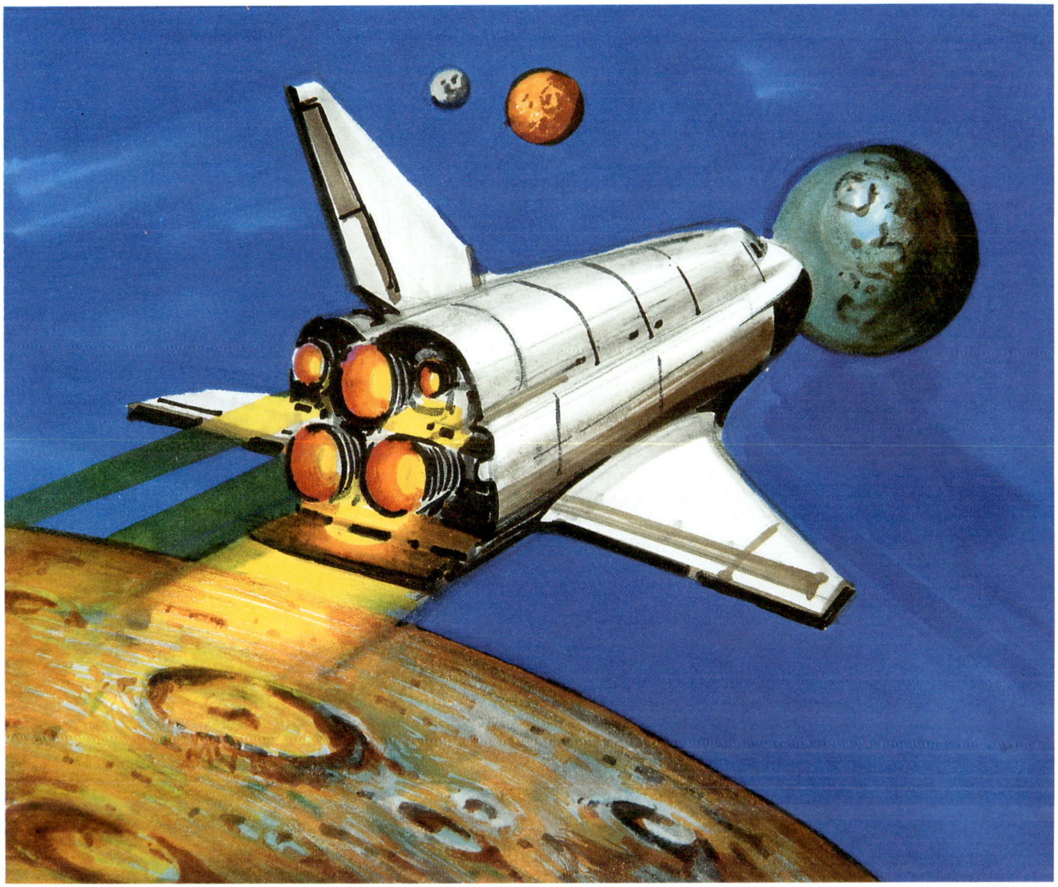

Advanced projects

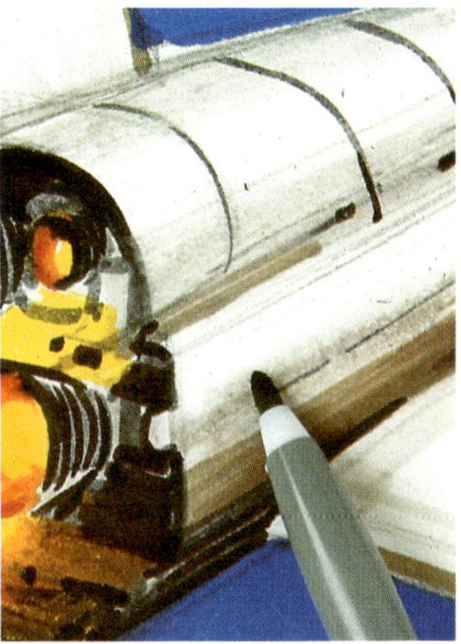

You can't gradate with a marker by pressing harder on the paper, as you can with pencils. You have to use different tones and blend them together using the lightest tone.

Continue to work the colours so that they blend and gradate with others.

Darken the shadows of the asteroid and paint a yellow line at the back of the reactors, to add more light to the picture.

Now you have finished the project, you should have a picture to be proud of.

Glossary

box. The first lines of a drawing. The name comes from boxes or geometric shapes (squares, rectangles, cubes, circles, etc), which are drawn to position the shapes in a picture.

cool colours. The colours in the colour wheel between green and violet, including both these colours.

felt. The material used for the wicks of markers, which absorbs the ink.

gradation. A gradual step from a dark tone to a lighter one, or vice versa.

lead pencil. This is the common pencil. Lead pencils vary in hardness, from 9H (the hardest), through HB and F (which are medium hard), to 8B (the softest).

perspective. A set of rules which make a drawing on the flat surface of a piece of paper look three-dimensional.

range. A group of tones of one colour.

reserving. Leaving white or light-coloured areas in a drawing uncoloured. The white of the paper creates a highlight in these areas.

sizing up. A basic rule which helps you to draw a subject accurately on paper.

transparent colours. Colours which do not cover the colour underneath. Mixes are done by putting colours on top of each other.

tone. Colour intensity or strength, which ranges from the lightest to the darkest.

warm colours. The colours in the colour wheel between crimson and light yellow, including both these colours.

watercolour. A painting technique in which the colours are diluted with water (see Learn to Paint with Watercolour in this series).